HIEBERTS'
Gluten-Free
Cooking

*195 Gluten-Free favorites from the
George and Betty Hiebert family*

ISBN 978-193375329-4

Design: Grace Troyer
Cover Photograph: Wesley Yoder — Recipe for Cream Puffs on the cover found on page 181

First Printing January 2013   5 м
Second Printing July 2013   5 м

Carlisle Press
WALNUT CREEK

2673 Township Road 421
Sugarcreek, OH 44681
800.852.4482

Meet the Hieberts

We are George and Betty Hiebert and live with our family near the city of Grande Prairie in northern Alberta, Canada. We are so thankful for twenty-nine years of marriage. Our oldest daughter Nicole (27) is married to Benjamin Bergen and they live about twenty minutes from the family home. Benjamin and Nicole enjoy music, reading and studying together, and using their teaching gifts in the local church. Michelle (24), Brianne (19), Kaitlyn (17), Matthew (14), Melissa (13), and Emily (11) are at home, keeping busy with homeschooling, writing, teaching, music, and household duties. We also have a hobby farm and enjoy our twelve goats, two sheep, one goose, growing rabbit population, frequent cats, and two dogs. There is much laughter and discussion in our home and we love to show hospitality—and enjoy being able to be a "safe haven" for gluten-intolerant friends. Our greatest love and passion, however, is in knowing and loving Jesus Christ—our Lord, our Redeemer, and our Friend. The focus of our life revolves around getting to know Him better and serving Him each day.

Matthew · Brianne · Benjamin & Nicole · George & Betty · Emily · Michelle · Melissa · Kaitlyn

iv

Introduction

For someone who has grown up in a home where gluten-free cooking and baking is an integral part of daily life, it is almost difficult to understand the helplessness that a newly diagnosed celiac or gluten-intolerant person feels. I mean, going gluten-free is *easy*. I do it all the time. I have done it now for over fourteen years.

Well, actually, it's not so very easy. For people who have lived the majority of their lives savoring the smell and flavor of freshly baked whole wheat bread...who have always considered a can of Campbell's tomato soup a necessity for a good casserole...who have always thickened their sauces and gravies with wheat flour...who have never even *dreamed* of reading the labels on their soy sauce and seasonings...who don't even know of any other flour options than all-purpose flour...who love the sticky deliciousness of Grandma's cinnamon rolls...who are used to just picking up a burger in town for a quick lunch...no, going gluten-free is not a simple task.

And neither is it very appealing to the wheat-adjusted taste buds! Perhaps you feel as though you are saying good-bye to all of your favorite foods, and think that you will have to live on rice crackers, vegetables, and flavorless meat for the rest of your life. You've tried the store-bought version of gluten-free bread and are tempted to despair when you think of eating that for years to come.

Or maybe you are enthused and eagerly ready to launch into this new lifestyle…but don't know where to start. Perhaps your doctor handed you a little pamphlet about the diet and directed you to a health-food store, but you still have so many questions. Simply put, the gluten-free lifestyle is completely different than what you have experienced so far—and you'd like some experienced help.

Over the years our family has been asked many times for our recipes and for help in starting a gluten-free diet, and many packages of photocopied pages have been sent in the mail. Now all those recipes and all those tips are compiled into one book…and we are so excited to be able to offer it to a wider audience.

We are not (by any stretch of the imagination!) cooking and baking extraordinaires, but we hope we can be of some practical and down-home help to you. You may just be starting into the gluten-free lifestyle or you may have been on the diet for a while—or, while being gluten-tolerant yourself, you may have friends on the gluten-free diet that you would like to be able to cook and bake for. Whatever the case, this cookbook will provide you with helpful ideas, real-life stories, and tried-and-true recipes.

Hieberts' Gluten-Free Cooking was a family effort. All the Hiebert ladies were involved in testing, compiling, and editing the recipes, and Kaitlyn, Brianne, and Nicole spent hours typing out each recipe. Mom and I did the bulk of the story/tip writing. But beyond those practical details, this cookbook represents years of daily cooking and baking…of experimentation and conversion from wheat to gluten-free…of flops and successes…of memories of working together in the kitchen and of home-cooked meals eaten and enjoyed as a family…

If this cookbook had a dedicatory page, there would be no doubt as to who would have the honor. My maternal grandmother, Liz Rempel (1935-2008), was truly the pioneer in our family's journey.

Her expertise in baking, her willingness to try new recipes, and her hard work in the kitchen to supply her granddaughters with what they needed for their celiac diet has left a treasured legacy for us. How she would have enjoyed seeing this cookbook—which includes a number of her original recipes, many of which are still our favorites. She truly was our inspiration and greatest support, and we thank the Lord for her!

We hope that you will find encouragement and help in the following pages and that through our story and recipes you will discover that going gluten-free is not as hard or unsavory as you may have thought. All the best in your gluten-free endeavors!

Michelle Hiebert
Valhalla Centre, Alberta
October 2012

Table of Contents

The Journey

I love being a mom. The Lord has blessed me and my husband George with seven children, and our years of training and teaching them has been an adventure. There have been challenges, but there have also been blessings along the way—many blessings—and I would not trade motherhood for any career out of the home.

Part of being a mother is looking out for the health and well-being of my family. I grew up on a farm. Fresh vegetables and home-baked goods were normal. My siblings and I enjoyed good health when we were growing up, with no serious ailments or conditions to be dealt with.

As I began having children and raising my own family, I didn't expect that there would be any major health issues to deal with.

Our first daughter, Nicole, was born in 1985. She was small at birth and very colicky for the first three months, but other than that she seemed healthy. As time went on, however, we noticed that she was quite small for her age. I brought this to the attention of our family doctor, who dismissed my concerns on the basis of the fact that my husband and I were not large people. Nicole had gained well in the first year of her life but weighed only 21 pounds at age 3. She also had stomach cramps which would cause her to double up in pain. The doctor dismissed them as probable flu symptoms. Nicole was a very passive child and lacking in energy. I remember her having to rest halfway up the stairs when she had to go upstairs in our house. She always wanted to be carried when we went to the park located next to our yard. I finally insisted that something was wrong when I once again brought Nicole in to see our doctor. A blood test was taken, and the next day at suppertime my doctor called, telling me to be at the Children's Hospital first thing the next morning.

Months of tests and procedures followed that were very uncomfortable and traumatic for Nicole. The doctors ignored my appeals to test for celiac disease. Nicole was not experiencing diarrhea—the classic symptom of celiac disease—so they would not investigate that possibility, even though celiac disease was on both my mother and father's side of the family. Finally after five months, they had exhausted all their tests and agreed to test for celiac disease. Nicole was sedated and a biopsy was done to look at the villi in her upper intestine. Even though it all happened while she was very young, Nicole has vivid memories of that time:

"I was only three years old when I was diagnosed with celiac disease. Barely three. I doubt most people have as many vivid memories as I do of such a young age. Trauma will do that, you know. And after three months of tests, one is bound to experience a measure of trauma. My mind has stored a number of incidents that were better left forgotten. I remember lying on a hard, narrow cot or bed of some kind (although it seems more like a stretcher to my memory) in a semi-darkened room. Across my chest and down along my body were several thick black straps holding me still. Slightly to the side of my range of vision was a big red EXIT sign. I was crying. Sobbing. Beside me sat my mother, pregnant at the time. She was also crying. To this day, I wonder if that scene was

shortly before my biopsy. I don't know.

"The second memory I have is sitting with my mother in the waiting room of the hospital. She was crying again. I have since been told that I had just refused to drink a very bitter medicine of some kind. Well, the medical community has their ways to circumnavigate obstinacy of that sort. A medical team with a child's wheelchair suddenly appeared in the waiting room. I was whisked away from my crying mother and wheeled down a long white hallway into a large windowless room. I was laid down on my back on a hard table. Two or three men and women in green scrubs stood at the wall with their backs to me, preparing something. I remember one of them telling me that they would give me a treat if I would stop crying. What happened next is forever impressed on my mind. They gathered around my bed—a circle of masked faces. I was held down, my face was tipped up, and a tube was forced up my nose and down my throat. My last memory is hearing my own terrified screams before my mind goes blank. The medicine, I believe, was deposited directly into my stomach. I don't recall any treat being given to me. But then, I hadn't kept my part of the deal either.

"My third memory takes place in the kitchen of our home. I was an early bird and would usually be up and about while my trusting parents slumbered on. I was quite used to being left to myself in the still hours of the early morning. Well, this particular morning, still in my pajamas and mussed hair, I had dragged a chair to the pantry to help myself to some cold cereal. With the cereal in my hands, I stood riveted in the pantry door as a terrific rumpus took place in the hallway. A moment later, Daddy stood swaying slightly in the doorway, still in his pajamas, with mussed hair, and squinting in the light of the kitchen. 'You can't eat!' he blurted hastily. 'More tests today!' "

Well, the big day came to hear the results. We sat in front of the specialist, who told us that the test was inconclusive, but he recommended starting a gluten-free diet. I asked him when I should start. He said immediately. I felt a sense of panic. What could she eat?

Back in 1988 the selection of gluten-free goods was *so* limited. Nicole ate a lot of rice cakes. The cookies and cakes I tried to bake for her crumbled in her hands. The gluten-free bread we bought was dry and tough.

I had an aunt and a cousin who had been diagnosed as celiacs years before, so recipes were shared, and Nicole's selection of gluten-free products grew and improved.

Back in those early days a man in Calgary was selling gluten-free products out of the basement of his home. His wife was celiac, and he developed a business which eventually moved to a store. We appreciated his help as we adjusted to a gluten-free diet.

Another wonderful blessing was my mother. She was an excellent baker, and now used all of her skills to change regular recipes to gluten-free ones by trying different measurements of rice flour and potato starch to make jelly rolls, moonlight cake, and other special goodies for her granddaughter. We still use her recipes and are so thankful for her efforts to make the transition to gluten-free eating for Nicole much easier.

Nicole now had to bring food with her wherever she went. At birthday parties she would come carrying not just a gift for the guest of honor but also a container with her own pizza, hot dog, or sandwich as well as a cupcake or two for dessert.

I don't recall Nicole complaining or feeling sorry for herself. We never allowed pity parties but rather reminded her how much better her health was, and how thankful we were that the doctor had found out what was wrong. Making separate food for her was expected and normal. We as parents never complained about it or resented it. I believe our attitude affected hers.

A friend once told me she thought that having a condition like celiac disease was actually a blessing for Nicole. At a young age Nicole had to be different, to stand alone and not do what everyone else did. Priscilla believed this would help Nicole in the future. She would be prepared and experienced in being different and standing alone for convictions in her Christian faith. I believe her perspective was accurate.

We had to learn much in those early days. Up until Nicole was diagnosed I had never looked at the ingredient list of anything I bought. Now, I carefully read every label on the foods I bought. Favorite and convenient canned soups couldn't be used anymore. In fact, most processed foods were a problem.

The Canadian Celiac Association was a great help in those first years after diagnosis. Their newsletters were full of helps, recipes, and ingredients that we should be aware of that may contain gluten.

In the 1990s celiac disease was fairly unknown. Because of having relatives with this condition we were more aware of it than many people. My cousin who was diagnosed as an infant was told that he would outgrow the disease and for his teen years started eating gluten with no side effects. Later, in his 20s, he started having health issues again and returned to a gluten-free diet.

Another interesting thing happened when we met a family a number of years ago and started spending time together. One evening when we were having supper together the father left after the meal and was in the restroom for a long time. We were concerned, but his wife said this often happened. He frequently felt sick after eating. In the course of our discussion she mentioned that she wondered if it had anything to do with a disease he had had as an infant. The doctors had told him he had outgrown it, and it wouldn't cause him any more trouble. We quickly shared that if it was celiac disease he had as an infant he most definitely had not outgrown it. The doctors in those years were wrong. Teenagers often did not show symptoms, but the disease remained. The family changed to a gluten-free diet for this man very shortly after that. It was in fact celiac disease that he had been diagnosed with as a baby.

Eating gluten-free was not always easy, as we learned just how careful we needed to be. A week or two after Nicole was diagnosed with celiac disease, our family stopped at a restaurant and ordered fried chicken. Mmm—bread coating—well, we would just remove the skin and it should be okay. We were wrong. Nicole threw up shortly after and we realized that eating gluten-free was much more serious than we thought.

Even though we read labels carefully and although all ingredients are supposed to be listed by Canadian law, Nicole did eat a cheese spread once that didn't have gluten on the ingredient list and yet she was very sick within twenty minutes of ingesting it. We became very picky about processed foods—the less ingredients the better. Over the last number of years eating gluten-free is *so* much easier. Health food stores cater to the gluten-free eater and regular grocery stores carry certified gluten-free products.

Within weeks of changing to a gluten-free diet we were noticing changes in our daughter. For three years we had a very passive and quiet little girl. Now her energy levels multiplied. She was loud, active, and sometimes naughty. In other words, she was now normal.

Hiebert's Gluten-Free Cooking

We actually had been living with a little girl who was slowly starving to death. Although she had been a good eater, her body simply could not absorb the nutrients she needed. Now that gluten had been removed from her diet, her intestines were healing and she was getting the nutrition her body had been craving.

It was like having a completely new child come to live with us. The difference in behavior and personality was dramatic. At times when Nicole was exceptionally noisy and rowdy, George and I would look at each other and suggest, "Should we give her some gluten?" Of course we were joking. Having a healthy, active child was a blessing and we were very thankful for her good health. It was, however, a great adjustment for her parents.

Physically, she thrived. Within six months of changing to a gluten-free diet, she had gained twelve pounds and had grown six inches. At a follow-up appointment with the specialist at the Children's Hospital he agreed (finally) that she really did have celiac disease. Her growth over that first year after the diet change proved her condition far better than all their blood work and tests.

Over the years, as the Lord gave us more children, we were faced with more health challenges. Our second daughter was not thriving and was very small for her age. Her immunity was very poor. Rather than putting her through the trauma of tests in the medical system, I decided to just try her on the diet for six months. If we saw noticeable differences we would assume that she was celiac. If there were no changes in her condition, we would look for other issues. Michelle did very well after the change to a gluten-free diet. Other children came along with various health challenges—tiredness, stomachaches, bedwetting. The gluten-free diet has helped each one of them. At this point in time, all six of our daughters eat gluten-free, and I try to eat gluten-free most of the time. We have found that two of our daughters are very sensitive to gluten. The others can eat a meal where gluten has been mistakenly added and not show obvious side effects. The other two react very quickly. It can show itself in stomachaches, diarrhea, or vomiting. Another obvious side effect of gluten contamination is severe mood swings.

One daughter was having a very difficult day, and after ruling out sickness or hormonal issues, we started evaluating any possible gluten contamination. We went through the last twenty-four hours of meals and snacks with no clue as to what the problem might be. Suddenly she remembered that she had drunk a root beer the night before. We quickly retrieved the can. Sure enough, there was gluten in it! Pop? Who would think about checking pop! But now we know.

Celiac disease is actually the best disease to have, though. Even with the difficulties of maintaining it at times, we are *so* thankful that this is the disease our family has to deal with. Celiac disease requires no surgery and no drugs. If we are strict with our diet we will enjoy very good health with no limitations on our lifestyle.

I believe our family is healthier because of the gluten-free diet. We became aware of what was in the food we bought (and were sometimes appalled!). As a result we started buying foods with less additives, less preservatives, and less colorings. Since gluten-free items were hard to find we began making sauces, dressings, and soups from scratch. It took more time, but we were confident that they were gluten-free and we knew that they were healthier.

Our journey with celiac disease has now been almost twenty-five years long. We usually don't even think much about it anymore.

Living with the gluten-free diet comes quite easily and naturally. We are very thankful for all the helps we've received along the way and hope that this cookbook will be a help to others who are on their own journey of gluten-free eating.

Betty Hiebert
Valhalla Centre, Alberta
October 2012

What We Have Learned

Practical Aspects of the Gluten-Free Lifestyle

Over the course of the past twenty-five years, we have learned much (sometimes by trial and error!) about how to "do" this gluten-free thing. It's second nature to us now…but we understand that for many just embarking on this journey, there is potentially a host of questions—and perhaps an overwhelmed feeling of helplessness as you think of all the necessary changes. Perhaps some of the things we have experienced and learned will help you!

Eating Out

You can imagine our joy in finding restaurants that know about the gluten-free diet. Gone are the days of calling the chef to our table and explaining carefully Nicole's diet and that he would need to clean his grill and not allow any wheat crumbs at all to touch her food. Often now when we tell the waitress about the need for gluten-free food she hands us a special menu just for the gluten-free eater!!

Of course, there are exceptions to this, such as the time when the waiter was very careful to eliminate the gravy from the turkey, but then served the turkey on two slices of wheat bread! Or the French-speaking waitress in a Quebec restaurant who didn't know what "flour" was. To this day, we aren't sure if she thought we meant "floor" or "flower." What we do know is that we ended up sticking to the safe part of the menu: side salads!

Eating at Other People's Homes

It can seem overwhelming and discouraging to tell others what we *cannot* eat, so we usually try to share what we *can* eat. Most people are very surprised at the great variety of choices that are ours. We try to give suggestions if they are very tentative in cooking for us. We make sure to tell them that all fresh fruits and vegetables are fine and that all unprocessed meats are also fine. One simple but delicious gluten-free menu choice is a roast or chicken dinner with potatoes, carrots, and onions. We just ask our hostess to read to us the labels of any seasonings they may add and then ask them to use cornstarch to thicken the gravy. If their menu includes pasta we offer to bring a bag of gluten-free rice or corn pasta and help them make that part of the meal. Arriving early to be on hand to read labels and answer questions is always appreciated. How about desserts? Fresh fruit or a gluten-free cake mix with whipped cream are delicious options.

Some of our friends excel in cooking for us because of choosing the gluten-free diet for themselves. When we arrive for a meal or for a few days' visit, they supply everything we need for gluten-free eating, including gourmet-style meals and snacks. What a treat!

But even most of our friends who are not on the gluten-free diet have learned how to cook gluten-free. We always offer to bring gluten-free bread or desserts, knowing that not everyone can bake gluten-free or even has gluten-free flours in the home. We have faced challenges, however; one being when dear, well-meaning people think that as long as the baking is made with *white* flour, it is wheat-free, which of course is not true! Nicole shares another challenge:

"Perhaps one of the greatest dangers to a celiac comes from well-meaning people who give the impression of being knowledgeable about your dietary needs. You feel like you should be safe with the foods they prepare for you, and besides, they might take offense if you question their hard efforts.

"When we were out for supper one evening, I was presented with a muffin which the hostess assured me was gluten-free. That night I woke up with severe stomach cramps and vomiting. In the back of my mind, I suspected that 'gluten-free' muffin, but didn't know for sure until some time later when we inadvertently learned that if our hostess didn't have quite enough gluten-free flour while she was baking, she would simply top off the measurement with wheat flour.

"Oh.

"From then on, I never ate anything that came from her kitchen unless it was from a store-bought, certified gluten-free mix."

Most people, however, are very careful when they cook for us. They ask lots of questions and read labels to us over the phone to make sure their food will be safe. Some have even gone on the Internet to do research on the diet. Others find a safe recipe that works and then prepare it whenever we come over—like Auntie Karen's signature Spanish rice dish—and we enjoy it every time! Nicole has come up with an information sheet that she hands out to anyone who is interested in knowing more about how to cook for her. The church fellowship that she and her husband are part of now does an excellent job of cooking gluten-free items for her.

Don't be afraid to tell your hosts about the need for gluten-free food. We made a mistake one time as we headed to a stranger's home for supper while on our long trip in 2005. We thought the girls could just eat salad or vegetables, so why bother the hostess, whom we had never met? We were wrong. She had spent the day making lasagne—a lot of it. When she found out about our gluten-free diet she was very disappointed. She now had all of this lasagne we couldn't eat, and to top it off she was fully aware of the gluten-free diet and would have made gluten-free lasagne for the girls had she only known! We learned our lesson!

Traveling

Our family has traveled a fair bit. We live many hours from our family and make long trips to visit our loved ones. On the way we have to be prepared to be creative in our food choices. It can be quite a hunt to find gluten-free products in small towns or gas station stores. The local grocery store, however, usually has fruit or veggie trays. Cheese sticks or gluten-free pepperoni sticks supply the needed protein and a box of gluten-free rice crackers fill out the meal (we usually keep a good supply of these in the van).

In 2005 our family took a three-and-a-half-month field trip across Canada and the United States. What a wonderful adventure! Gluten-free eating was part of the challenge. We bought pre-made mixes for bread, cookies, and cakes. Gluten-free cereals were usually available. And if all else failed, rice cakes with peanut butter or mayonnaise and processed ham filled us up. After so many of these lunches the children now have a hard time eating processed ham and we haven't bought rice cakes for years! Some fast-food restaurants offered baked potatoes and salads. We were able to enjoy these as well. We occasionally even splurged and bought pre-made pizzas, burritos, and other items in the gluten-free freezer section of large grocery stores. An expensive treat!

Nicole's testimony: *"The real challenge was staying at different homes. Most people were very accommodating and even eager to cook food we* could eat. Some people had never heard of gluten. Others assumed they understood our dietary needs and assured us that the food was fine, but when it came to the meal in question, we would find ourselves face to face with an ingredient we couldn't eat. Like the time an apparently gluten-free casserole was topped with a layer of cornflakes. We didn't know our hosts, so we discreetly scraped off the cornflakes and prayed that God would protect our bodies from an adverse reaction.

"It is still amazing to me that during the entire trip, I never once felt the effects of gluten contamination. I believe the Lord was very gracious to us, for there were times when I simply had to eat what was set before me even when we weren't completely sure that it was totally safe. Actually, by the end of the trip, I had lowered my guards. Maybe I wasn't as sensitive as we assumed, I thought. Maybe there was less risk of contamination than we had always believed.

"My delusion was short lived. Less than three weeks after our return home, I helped myself to some taco meat at a potluck, and within ten minutes I was feeling miserable. An hour later, I was prostrate with a severe reaction to a gluten ingredient in the taco seasoning. Any mercy that had been extended to me during the trip was over! It was time to resume the vigilance which should be second nature to any celiac."

If we go on shorter holidays for a week or two we will make up our own mixes for muffins, bread, or pancakes. Then when we are staying at the homes of friends we can bake up some items to take along to the next stop.

Gluten-free baking is best eaten fresh, which makes traveling a bit challenging. Bread freezes well. We slice it before we freeze it, so we just take out pieces as we need them. Keeping it frozen, however, can be difficult as ice packs thaw in the cooler and the bread isn't as nice. We have found that cookies and muffins do dry out quickly, so being able to bake along the way is necessary though sometimes time consuming and inconvenient.

A Note on Dairy Allergies

Brianne shares: *"Often people who are gluten-intolerant or celiacs find themselves not able to handle other foods as well, two common culprits being corn and dairy. I have never been able to handle dairy very well, getting a stuffy nose after a meal with a large amount of dairy or a cup of milk. But three or four years ago I began noticing my symptoms increasing. I would get a severe stomachache, accompanied by a stuffy nose, after consuming large amounts of dairy. Or I'd have a cough and a mucus buildup in the back of my throat. I've struggled with sinus infections for the past several years, as well as recurring earaches. I began to limit my dairy consumption, cutting out ice cream and cheese and obvious dairy foods. Finally I got a milk goat and really began to change my diet, cutting out all dairy products possible: milk in cereal, butter on toast, etc. Within two weeks I could tell a difference: I could finally breathe through my nose at night. My family said they could see the difference on me, as my sinuses were no longer swollen.*

"I can tell almost immediately if a food I've eaten has dairy in it; even a hot vegetable with butter makes me get all congested. Because I react so strongly and quickly, I've learned to ask what someone is serving ahead of time so that I can bring my own food if needed, like dairy-free mashed potatoes or goat-milk cheese or a dessert. If I'm in a situation where I haven't brought my own stuff and there's nothing dairy-free, I'll occasionally take a small portion, but most often I'll just go without. The side effects outweigh the pleasure. It has taken a lot of adjustment and sometimes sacrifice, but it has been worth it. With my milk from my goat, I've been able to enjoy pudding, cheese, and yogurt, as well as cream gravies and milk shakes. When I bake, I'll use either water or

half-water/half-goat's milk in place of regular milk. Whenever I can, I'll use oil instead of butter. I also use margarine, looking for brands that are both gluten- and lactose-free. The foods I've missed the most are whipped cream and ice cream, as my goat doesn't give enough cream to make those. Cool Whip has been my alternative, even though it has a trace amount of milk in it. Recently I've discovered coconut milk ice cream, which I use for a special treat, and coconut milk ice cream bars. One of my sisters, who tries to avoid a lot of dairy, uses almond milk.

"Often I'll hear people talking and I'll think, That person needs to go off dairy. He/she is terribly stuffed up. Often a dairy allergy will hide itself in the sinuses, making itself less obvious to most people, but when those people actually go off of dairy, others around them can hear the difference in the way they talk. Recurring sinus and ear infections, constant pressure in the sinuses and ears, continual mucus buildup—all of these are symptoms of a dairy intolerance. The thought of eliminating dairy from your diet might be scary and overwhelming, but I can say that it is worth it. And there's still plenty you can eat!"

Oats

When Nicole was initially diagnosed with celiac disease we were told that oats contained a small amount of gluten, most likely from contamination in processing facilities. Different countries have made varying conclusions and recommendations in what they tell celiacs to do with oats.

We did give Nicole oats for a number of years. Our specialist said it would be fine. When she was around 7-8 years of age though, her complaints of stomachaches led us to decide to remove oats from her diet. The stomachaches disappeared. In her adult years Nicole started eating oats again, but she now eats only pure, uncontaminated oats (available at health-food stores) a few times a week. It is more expensive, but in order to maintain optimum health she is very careful to only eat uncontaminated oats.

Nicole shares: *"Oats and celiacs have made for a controversial combination for years, but the end of the controversy is in sight. In Canada, oats is considered acceptable for celiacs if it is pure, uncontaminated oats. You see, the biggest problem with regular oats is that it is processed alongside other grains which spell trouble for celiacs. In the entire process, from the field to the package, pure oats has been kept from all contamination with gluten grains. Even so, the Canadian Celiac Association recommends that celiacs only consume a limited amount of oats. As a result, we only have oatmeal twice a week in our home. Since it's our favorite hot cereal, Mondays and Thursdays are special mornings!"*

Cross Contamination

A very important aspect of the gluten-free lifestyle is the need to be very careful about cross contamination. If you use the same utensils/pans/dishes/measuring cups for gluten-free baking as you do for wheat baking, *make sure you wash them carefully before using them!* This may be one of the biggest adjustments for some bakers and cooks who are used to simply dusting off the counter after cutting wheat bread or shaking off the baking sheets and putting them back into the cupboard without washing. For a gluten-intolerant person, "dusting off" or "shaking off" is not sufficient. A thorough wash is necessary.

Another thing to be aware of is how you handle your margarine, butter, mayonnaise, jam, and peanut butter. While these are gluten-free products in and of themselves (check the peanut butter: avoid the brands that have powdered/icing sugar in the ingredient list, since not all powdered/icing sugar is gluten-free), if they have been dipped into by knives used on wheat bread they are no longer safe for the gluten-intolerant person. Either set aside a special gluten-free butter/jam/mayonnaise/etc. jar or dish or make sure to always use a spoon to serve (and don't use that spoon to spread a piece of wheat bread!).

Oh…and don't use a piece of wheat bread to keep your brown sugar soft. Purchasing a special sugar softener is a much better option!

Ingredients to Avoid

The headache of explaining to others…while wheat, barley, wheat starch, etc., are easy enough to identify, the *real* challenge comes when you try explaining that dextrose is fine, maltodextrin isn't, unless it specifies that it is derived from corn, and also don't forget that malt flavoring, malt extract, and malt syrup are no-nos, but malt vinegar and malt sugar are perfectly safe! There definitely comes a point when it's much easier to provide one's own food!

The other option is to make up a written list and give it to your keen and eager friends who are just waiting to bake and cook for you. Here is the list we hand out if we are asked:

When scanning labels and choosing baking flours, here are the main ingredients that a gluten-intolerant person should avoid at all times:

- Modified food starch (unless it specifies corn/soy/rice)
- Hydrolyzed plant protein (unless it specifies corn/soy/rice)
- Hydrolyzed vegetable protein (unless it specifies corn/soy/rice)
- Maltodextrin (unless it specifies corn/soy/rice)
- Dextrin (unless it specifies corn/soy/rice; take note that dextrose is fine)
- Malt flavoring (maltose and malt vinegar are fine)
- Wheat (starch and flour)
- Barley

- Rye
- Spelt
- Kamut
- Semolina
- Triticale
- Bulgur
- Oats (unless pure and uncontaminated)

Another questionable ingredient is mono- and di-glycerides. Nicole shares her experience: "Have you ever seen that tongue-twisting ingredient called mono- and di-glycerides? It's found in most ice cream. It's a tricky ingredient because it can be derived from a gluten-free source, but it can also be derived from a gluten source. The contamination is so slight it doesn't result in out-and-out symptoms for me. What it will do, though, is send me into a mood swing for 24 -36 hours after consuming the dessert. Although some brands of ice cream clearly identify their product as gluten-free, they seem to think this gives them permission to charge higher prices. Other brands might be gluten-free, but they don't specify it. So…what results is a gamble and a joke. My husband and I are at a friend's house, and they pass the bucket of ice cream to us to check the ingredients. All looks good except for that suspicious mono- and di-glycerides. We exchange a look with raised eyebrows. Is it worth risking a cry the following day? I usually decide that it is. In most cases, everything is just fine. In the rare instances when it isn't, my husband gets greeted in the evening of the next day by an overwhelmed and teary wife—so we both pay the price of the gamble!"

Gravies and Thickeners

We make gluten-free gravy from the drippings of chicken or beef. For added flavor, we add salt and pepper as well as sage (to chicken or turkey gravy). Gluten-free bouillon cubes and powder are available at health-food stores, and if we have some on hand we will use it. For thickening, cornstarch is our favorite choice. We make a smooth paste with cornstarch and water and then whisk it into the boiling drippings. Allow it to boil for at least a minute so that the gravy is not starchy.

Easy Gluten-Free Lunches

We buy corn tortillas in bulk whenever we can. After they are heated (in frying pan, oven, or microwave), they are an easy and delicious choice for lunch. We fill them with whatever is in our fridge (leftovers, meats, vegetables, cheese, etc.) and serve them with mayonnaise, salsa, or sour cream. Always a favorite!

Our plain muffin recipe is very easy and quick to prepare. Fresh muffins with soup or sandwich ingredients make for a satisfying meal.

Gluten-Free Baking Tips

Gluten-free baking is a much more delicate art than wheat baking is. So if the recipe calls for two cups gluten-free flour, make sure you carefully measure out *two cups gluten-free flour*—not two heaping cups or two scant cups. Level out your measuring cup with a butter knife.

Gluten-free dough/batter can never be overworked; the longer it is beaten, the better the result will be.

Gluten-free bread baking is a completely different process than wheat bread baking. Do not expect to be able to knead your dough, because you won't have dough to knead! Unbaked gluten-free bread is more like muffin batter, to be spooned into the bread pans and spread with a spatula. Don't give in to the temptation to add more flour than the recipe specifies—if you do, the finished product will not be very delectable!

If you keep your gluten-free baking on the counter, make sure it is in an airtight container because gluten-free baking dries out much quicker than wheat baking does. Actually, don't even allow your gluten-free baking to completely cool after it comes out of the oven. With the exception of bread (which cuts better when allowed to cool), we usually bag our baking while it is still warm. It stays fresher longer that way.

Unlike wheat baking, gluten-free baking normally dries out if it gets cold. So don't refrigerate your bread, cookies, cakes, or muffins. It's best to either leave your baking on the counter in an airtight container (if you plan to eat it within the next day or two) or to freeze it. We have found that if we freeze our baking (such as cookies and muffins) *immediately*, it remains moist much longer. A cousin of ours who is also on the gluten-free diet bags her baking while it's still hot and then immediately puts it in the freezer.

Xanthan gum is a critical ingredient if you want to find success in your gluten-free baking. One-half to one teaspoon of xanthan gum per cup of gluten-free flour in a recipe will change the finished result from a gritty, crumbly mess to a moist, almost-like-wheat treat. This necessary (albeit expensive) product can be purchased at health-food stores, and we store ours in an airtight container in the freezer to lengthen its shelf life. We used to use guar gum, but found that xanthan gum gave us a better product.

Using Leftover Gluten-Free Bread

When we have leftover, dried-out gluten-free bread we put it to one of the following uses:

1. Put the pieces in your food processor/blender and make bread crumbs. Freeze and use in hamburgers, meat loaves, or other recipes.

2. Cut bread into cubes to make gluten-free croutons. Melt butter and add your favorite spices (we add a mixture of garlic powder, oregano, basil, thyme, salt, and parsley). Mix together with bread cubes in bowl and spread on pans. Bake in 400° oven. Stir occasionally until crisp. Cool and freeze for use in salads or soups.

Crumbly Cookies and Cakes

Sometimes gluten-free cookies and cakes turn out rather crumbly—especially when the baker forgets to add the xanthan gum. We break up these "flops" and then bag and freeze them. They work nicely over ice cream or as a base for a pudding dessert.

Gluten-Free Flour Mix

In all of the recipes in this book we use one flour mix: what we refer to as gluten-free flour mix (two parts brown rice flour to one part tapioca starch). Although we have occasionally used other flours, we find that in our busy home, keeping everything simple is always best.

We usually buy 25-lb. bags of brown rice and grind our own flour with our Wonder Mill grinder. Sometimes we buy ready-ground brown rice flour in 25-lb. bags. This makes life simpler and our baking just a bit nicer, since commercially ground flour is finer than we can make it. We keep bags of flour in the freezer to avoid it going rancid. We buy 25–50-lb. bags of tapioca starch through bulk distributors. Tapioca starch is very fine and therefore extremely messy; just to forewarn you!

Every week we make a large tub of gluten-free flour mix, and then we are able to bake throughout the week whenever we need to without having to mix up a batch of gluten-free flour mix each time.

Adapting Wheat Recipes to Gluten-Free

The majority of the recipes in this cookbook were originally wheat recipes that our family altered and adjusted over the years. We have become quite adept at adapting recipes, and with practice you too may find that it is not so very hard. While all the recipes in this cookbook are already gluten-free (and therefore need no adjusting), there may come a time that you want to convert your favorite wheat recipes (such as cookies, muffins, and cakes—breads will not work as well) to gluten-free. Here are some tips as you experiment:

– for every cup of wheat/all-purpose flour in the original recipe, substitute one cup of gluten-free flour mix (two parts brown rice flour to one part tapioca starch)

–for every cup of gluten-free flour mix, add ½–1 teaspoon of xanthan gum

–if eggs are already in the recipe, add one extra egg

–beat the batter an extra amount—until well combined and smooth. Gluten-free batter should *not* remain lumpy!

All the best in your gluten-free baking endeavors!

And now on to the recipes!

A Few Basics

My Notes

Gluten-Free Flour Mix

2 parts brown rice flour

1 part tapioca starch

Mix well and store in airtight container.

White Sauce

2 Tbsp. butter

2 Tbsp. rice flour

¼ tsp. salt

1 cup milk

Melt butter in saucepan. Add the rice flour and salt, cooking and stirring until bubbly. Using a wire whisk, stir in the milk. Cook just until smooth and thickened. Makes slightly over 1 cup. For a thick sauce, increase butter and rice flour to 3 Tbsp. each. For a thin sauce, decrease butter and rice flour to 1 Tbsp. each.

Classic White Sauce

1 cup cold milk
1 Tbsp. cornstarch
2 Tbsp. butter
¼ tsp. salt
⅛ tsp. pepper

In small saucepan gradually stir milk into cornstarch until smooth. Add butter, salt, and pepper. Stirring constantly, bring to boil over medium heat; boil 1 minute to thicken.

Easy Cheese Sauce

A good substitute for processed cheese sauces.

Prepare Classic White Sauce (above). Stir 1 cup shredded cheddar cheese into prepared sauce until melted. Serve over broccoli, cauliflower, or baked potatoes.

Lemon Herb Sauce

Prepare Classic White Sauce (on preceding page). Stir 1 Tbsp. chopped fresh herbs or ¼ tsp. dried herbs (such as dill, basil, or parsley) and 1 Tbsp. lemon juice into prepared sauce. Serve over cooked vegetables, poultry, or seafood.

Taco Seasoning Mix

Makes 5 mixes; 3 Tbsp.=1 package chili/taco mix.

- ¼ cup gluten-free flour mix
- 2 Tbsp. chili powder
- ¼ cup onion powder
- 2 tsp. garlic powder
- 4 tsp. salt
- 4 tsp. paprika
- ½ tsp. cayenne pepper
- 2 tsp. sugar
- 2 tsp. cumin
- 2 tsp. oregano

Put everything in a blender, cover, and blend for 5 seconds or until powdery. Add more cayenne pepper if you prefer it hotter. Store in an airtight container for up to 6 months.

My Notes

Hieberts' Gluten-Free Cooking

Soups & Stews

My Notes

Cheddar Ham Chowder

This soup won raves at a church fellowship meal. ~Nicole

2 cups water
2 cups cubed potatoes
½ cup sliced carrots
½ cup sliced celery
¼ cup chopped onion
1 tsp. salt
¼ tsp. pepper
¼ cup butter
¼ cup rice flour
2 cups milk
2 cups shredded cheddar cheese
2 cups frozen corn
1½ cups cooked ham

In a large saucepan, bring water, potatoes, carrots, celery, onion, salt, and pepper to a boil. Reduce heat; cover and simmer 8–10 minutes or until vegetables are just tender. Remove from heat. Do not drain. Meanwhile, in another saucepan, melt butter and blend in the rice flour. Add milk. Cook and stir until thickened. Add cheese and stir until melted. Stir into undrained vegetables and return to heat. Add corn and ham. Heat thoroughly and serve.

Corn and Bean Chowder

One of my husband's favorite soups! ~ Nicole

¼ cup oil

2 cups sliced onions

2 garlic cloves, minced

4 cups corn (fresh or frozen), divided

4 cups chicken broth (I use 4 cups boiling water and add 2 heaping tsp.
   of gluten-free chicken broth powder)

1 cup powdered milk

1½ cups cooked kidney beans

½ tsp. salt

In a large pot, sauté the onions and garlic in the oil. Add 3 cups of corn and the broth. Bring mixture to a boil and simmer until corn is tender. Puree the remaining corn in a blender. Add the pureed corn, powdered milk, beans, and salt to the pot. Bring soup almost to boiling, lower heat, and simmer for a few minutes. 6–8 servings.

Chicken Noodle Soup

4 servings

1 quart chicken broth

2 cups chopped carrots

2 cups chopped celery

1 tsp. salt

½ tsp. sugar

¼ tsp. pepper

1 tsp. gluten-free chicken bouillon powder

2 cups cooked, chopped chicken

gluten-free cooked spaghetti

Heat broth and vegetables to boiling. Simmer until vegetables are tender. Add seasonings and chicken. Just before serving, add spaghetti.

Chicken Rice Soup

6 servings

2 Tbsp. melted butter

1 carrot, chopped

1 onion, chopped

1 quart chicken broth

½ cup raw brown rice

2 chicken breasts, fried and cut up

1 Tbsp. gluten-free Spike seasoning (salt-free version is gluten-free)

1½ cups milk

1½ Tbsp. cornstarch

1 cup frozen peas

2 Tbsp. parsley, finely chopped

1 tsp. salt to taste

Sauté carrot and onion in butter. Cook rice in broth for 30–45 minutes. Combine broth, rice, chicken, onion, carrot, and Spike. Bring to a boil, reduce heat, and simmer until vegetables are tender. Mix cornstarch and milk together, then add to soup, stirring until thickened. About 5–7 minutes before serving, add peas, parsley, and salt.

Rosy Potato Soup

5 servings

- 1 large onion, chopped
- ¾ cup chopped celery
- 3 Tbsp. butter
- 1 Tbsp. rice flour
- ½–¾ tsp. salt
- 3 cups milk
- 3 medium potatoes, peeled, sliced, and cooked
- ½ Tbsp. dried parsley
- 1 Tbsp. paprika

In a large saucepan, sauté onion and celery in butter until tender. Stir in rice flour and salt until blended. Gradually add the milk. Bring to a boil; cook and stir for 2 minutes or until thickened and bubbly. Reduce heat. Add potatoes, parsley, and paprika. Heat through.

Pureed Potato Soup

This is a very satisfying soup that we have enjoyed for years!

4 Tbsp. butter

2 tsp. oil

2 cloves garlic, minced

1 large onion, chopped

4 cups celery

10 medium potatoes, cut into 1-inch squares

1 large squash, cut into ¼-inch squares

2 tsp. thyme

½ tsp. tarragon

1 tsp. sage

salt

dash of cayenne

10-12 cups water

Melt butter and heat oil. Add garlic, onion, and celery and sauté until they begin to wilt. Add potatoes, squash, and seasonings. Add water to cover vegetables. Bring to boil. Simmer while covered for 20 minutes or until veggies are soft. Cool slightly and puree in increments. Reheat gently, stirring so soup doesn't stick.

Split Pea Soup

Easy to make and a favorite.

> 2 cups green split peas
> 1 large can gluten-free tomato sauce

Boil split peas until soft. Blend in blender and pour back into the pot. Add tomato sauce, stir, and heat through. Serve with croutons or frozen corn and bread.

Taco Soup

Makes a Dutch-oven full—very popular!

> 1½ lbs. hamburger, browned and drained
> 4 cups whole kernel corn
> 4 cups pinto beans, cooked
> 1 (680 ml.) can gluten-free tomato sauce
> 2 cups gluten-free salsa
> 2–3 Tbsp. gluten-free taco seasoning (see taco seasoning recipe on page 29)

Mix all ingredients together and heat till warm or hot. Add water if necessary for thinner consistency. Serve over corn chips and top with grated cheese. Also good with a dollop of sour cream.

Beefy Tomato Soup

1 lb. ground beef
1 cup chopped onion
½ cup chopped celery
1 Tbsp. butter
13 oz. can gluten-free tomato paste
⅓ cup brown rice
1 tsp. salt
½ tsp. chili powder
1 bay leaf
5–6 cups water

Sauté beef, onion, and celery in butter until meat is browned. Stir in remaining ingredients; bring to a boil. Cover and simmer for 40 minutes. Remove bay leaf before serving.

Beef Stew

4–6 servings

   2 lbs. stewing beef, cut into 1-inch cubes
   2 Tbsp. cooking oil
   3 cups water
   1 large onion, chopped
   1 tsp. black pepper
   2 tsp. salt
   1½ tsp. garlic powder
   1 tsp. crushed rosemary
   1 tsp. dried oregano
   1 tsp. dried basil
   2 bay leaves
   2 (6 oz.) cans gluten-free tomato paste
   3 cups peeled, cubed potatoes
   2 cups sliced carrots
   1 large green pepper, chopped
   2 cups frozen peas
   2 cups frozen corn
   3 medium tomatoes, chopped

Brown meat in oil in a Dutch oven. Add water, onion, seasonings, and tomato paste. Cover and simmer for 2 hours or until meat is tender. Stir in potatoes, carrots, and green pepper; simmer for 30 minutes. Add additional water if necessary. Stir in remaining ingredients. Cover and simmer 20 minutes. Serve with fresh bread.

Slow-Cooker Beef Stew

2 stalks celery, diagonally sliced

3 cloves garlic, thinly sliced

1 medium onion, cut in large chunks

2 lbs. stewing beef

4 large carrots, diagonally sliced

10 medium potatoes, cut in chunks

1 Tbsp. gluten-free beef bouillon powder in 2 cups water

2 tsp. salt

½ tsp. pepper

2 bay leaves

Sauté celery, garlic, and onion with stewing beef in 1 tsp. olive oil until meat is lightly browned. Combine all ingredients in slow cooker. Cook on low for 8 hours or until done. Remove liquid from slow cooker to make gravy. Mix 1 Tbsp. beef bouillon powder with 1 cup of boiling water and add to liquid. When mixture boils, stir in 1 Tbsp. cornstarch which has been mixed in 1 cup of cold water. Bring gravy to a boil again, stirring with a whisk. Pour over stew and serve with freshly baked plain muffins and a salad.

Lori's Cider Stew

6–8 servings

2 lbs. beef stew meat, cut into 1-inch cubes

3 Tbsp. gluten-free flour

2 tsp. salt

¼ tsp. pepper

¼ tsp. thyme

3 Tbsp. oil

2 cups apple cider or apple juice

½ cup water

1–2 Tbsp. vinegar

3 medium potatoes, peeled and quartered

4 medium carrots, peeled and quartered

2 medium onions, sliced

1 stalk celery, sliced

Combine flour, salt, pepper, and thyme. Coat meat with flour mixture. In a Dutch oven, brown meat in oil. Drain off fat. Stir in apple juice, water, and vinegar. Bring to boiling. Reduce heat. Cover and simmer for 1¼ hours or until tender. Stir in vegetables. Cover and simmer 45–60 minutes more or until done.

Meat Loaf Stew

¼ cup water

5-6 medium potatoes, peeled and cut bite-sized

6 medium carrots, peeled and cut bite-sized

sprinkle of salt

sprinkle of pepper

1 large egg

⅓ cup ketchup

2 tsp. gluten-free beef bouillon powder

⅓ cup finely chopped onion

¼ tsp. thyme

¼ cup water

⅓ cup gluten-free bread crumbs

1 tsp. salt

¼ tsp. pepper

1½ lbs. ground beef

Pour first amount of water into slow cooker. Add potatoes and carrots; sprinkle with salt and pepper. Combine rest of ingredients in a bowl and mix well. Spread over potatoes and carrots. Cook on low for 8–10 hours or on high for 4–5 hours.

Salads & Dressings

My Notes

Sweet and Sour Lettuce Salad

torn lettuce

11 oz. mandarin orange segments or a fresh orange, peeled and
  cut into bite-sized pieces (optional)

¼ cup slivered almonds

1 Tbsp. + 1 tsp. sugar

Dressing:

¼ cup vegetable oil

1 Tbsp. honey

2 scant Tbsp. vinegar

½ tsp. salt

parsley

dash of pepper

Cook almonds and sugar over medium heat, stirring constantly, until sugar is melted and almonds are coated. Spread on a plate and cool, then break apart. Sprinkle over salad. Mix dressing well and pour over lettuce.

Waldorf Salad

4 crisp apples, unpeeled, chopped

4 stalks crisp medium celery, chopped

¼ generous cup walnuts, chopped

¼ generous cup pecans, chopped

½ cup raisins

1 (19 oz.) can pineapple chunks, drained

1 cup mayonnaise

3 tsp. honey

3 tsp. lemon juice

Mix first 6 ingredients. Combine with mayonnaise, honey, and lemon juice.

Seven-Layer Salad

lettuce/salad greens

1 cup thinly sliced celery

½ cup chopped green pepper

¼ cup sliced green onions

1 (12 oz.) package bacon, cut into 1-inch pieces, cooked

2 cups frozen green peas, thawed

1½ cups Miracle Whip

¾ cup shredded cheese

Place greens in large glass bowl. Layer celery, green pepper, onions, bacon, and peas over top. Spread Miracle Whip evenly over peas, covering the top completely and sealing to the edge of the bowl. Sprinkle with cheese. Cover and refrigerate 2–12 hours to blend flavors. Toss before serving if desired.

Grandma's 3-Layer Jell-O

Bottom:

2 packages gluten-free lime Jell-O

1 can crushed pineapple

Middle:

2 cups whipped cream (not too stiff)

1 (3 oz.) package gluten-free lemon Jell-O

¾ cup boiling water

1 (8 oz.) package cream cheese (room temperature)

¾ cup sugar

1 package gelatin

Top:

2 packages gluten-free red Jell-O (clear)

For bottom layer, mix Jell-O and pineapple. Pour into glass pan. For middle layer, combine Jell-O and gelatin. Add boiling water and stir until gelatin dissolves. Put cheese and sugar in different container,, and cream it together until smooth. Stir in cooled (lukewarm) gelatin mixture. Set in cold water and chill until it starts to set. Beat this mixture and add whipped cream. Beat until light and fluffy. Pour onto green layer (already set). Make sure edges are against glass. For top layer, cool and pour on middle layer.

Salmon Salad

4–6 cups uncooked gluten-free macaroni

2 tins salmon

½ cucumber, cut small

3 boiled eggs, peeled and chopped (optional)

Dressing:

¾ cup mayonnaise

1 tsp. honey

1 Tbsp. lemon juice

1 tsp. basil

1 tsp. thyme

Cook the macaroni and cool. Mash salmon with a fork. Combine the salmon, eggs, and cucumber with the pasta. Stir dressing together in cup, pour over pasta, and stir to coat. Add more mayonnaise and lemon juice if needed. On a hot day, we frequently serve this and a large fruit salad as our meal—simple and satisfying.

Grandma's Rice and Pineapple Salad

2 cups uncooked white rice

1 cup sugar

28 oz. crushed pineapple, drained

1 large container Cool Whip

Cook rice until tender. Drain rice and rinse well with cold water. Add sugar. Put in fridge overnight. Mix pineapple into rice. Stir in Cool Whip and serve.

Pineapple Sunshine Salad

3 cups pineapple juice

2 Tbsp. unflavored Knox gelatin

1 (19 oz.) can crushed pineapple, with juice

3 bananas, sliced

2 cups seedless grapes, cut in half

6 Tbsp. honey

In a small saucepan, whisk gelatin into 1½ cups of the pineapple juice. Let stand about five minutes while you mix the remaining pineapple juice, the crushed pineapple, bananas, and grapes in a large salad bowl. Heat the gelatin/pineapple juice to boiling while stirring constantly with wire whisk. Remove from heat and add the honey. Combine with the fruit in salad bowl. Stir well; cover and refrigerate until set. (This is a very flexible recipe. Experiment with other fruits like oranges and blueberries. Or substitute half the juice for orange juice. Healthy and yummy!)

Carrot Salad

10–15 carrots

raisins

mayo-honey dressing

Peel carrots if needed; shred. Mix with a few handfuls of raisins—how many depends on your family's tastes. Mix in dressing.

Poppy Seed Carrot Salad

10–15 carrots
4 tsp. poppy seeds
⅓ cup sunflower seeds
mayo/honey dressing

Shred the carrots on a small shred. Mix in a large bowl with seeds. Add dressing and stir well.

Pineapple Carrot Salad

10–15 carrots
1 (19 oz.) can crushed pineapple, pineapple tidbits, or rings cut in bite-sized pieces
3–4 apples
dried, sweetened cranberries (approx. ¼ cup)
mayo-honey dressing

Shred carrots and apples on a regular shred. Combine all ingredients in a large bowl.

Mayo-Honey Dressing

Our staple dressing for carrot salads and coleslaws.

> mayonnaise
> honey
> vinegar/lemon juice

To two or three spoonfuls of mayo, add honey and a little bit of vinegar or lemon juice to taste.

Cucumber Salad

> 3 large cucumbers, peeled and cut into a bowl
> 2 tsp. vinegar
> ½ cup mayonnaise
> salt and pepper to taste

Mix well. For a creamier salad, add some cream.

Herbed Mayonnaise Salad Dressing

1 cup mayonnaise

1 Tbsp. lemon juice

1 Tbsp. honey

2 tsp. basil

2 tsp. thyme

Mix well and store in refrigerator. If it thickens over time, add a little water before serving.

For a variation, omit the basil and thyme and add fresh or dried dill to taste.

French Salad Dressing

¾ cup vegetable oil

¼ cup vinegar

¼ cup honey

¼ cup ketchup

¼ tsp. salt

scant ⅛ tsp. garlic powder

Mix well and store in refrigerator.

Sweet and Sour Cream Salad Dressing

½ cup cream or milk

3 Tbsp. vinegar

1 Tbsp. sugar

¼ tsp. salt

Simple Thousand Island Dressing

1 cup mayonnaise

¼ cup ketchup

2 Tbsp. relish

1 tsp. parsley

salt and pepper to taste

My Notes

Meats & Main Dishes

My Notes

Scalloped Potatoes and Ham

6 servings

2–3 lbs. potatoes, peeled, diced, and cooked
1 lb. gluten-free sausage or ham, cooked and cubed

Sauce:
¼ cup butter, melted
⅓ cup rice flour
2 cups milk
1½ tsp. salt
dash pepper
½–¾ cup shredded cheese

Put potatoes and sausage in a casserole dish. Add a little onion if desired. For sauce, melt butter and add the rice flour. Stir, then add remaining ingredients except for the cheese. Cook and stir until it starts to thicken. Pour sauce over potatoes and sausage. Sprinkle cheese on top. Cover and bake at 350° for 1 hour.

Potatoes and Peas with Ham

4–6 servings

6–8 medium potatoes, scrubbed and quartered

4 green onions, snipped

1 cup frozen peas

2 Tbsp. butter

2 Tbsp. rice flour

½ cup reserved vegetable water

1 cup milk

salt and pepper to taste

1 cup cubed cooked ham

½ cup grated cheese

Cook potatoes in boiling salted water. When potatoes are just tender enough, add the green onions and frozen peas. Boil for a minute longer, then drain, reserving ½ cup of the liquid. Melt butter in a separate saucepan and add the rice flour, stirring until bubbly. Combine the vegetable liquid and milk, then add to butter and rice flour. Cook and stir until thickened. Add salt and pepper. Pour sauce over vegetables and add the ham and cheese. Heat through and serve.

Sweet and Sour Sausage Sauce

2¼ lbs. gluten-free sausage
1 cup brown sugar
1 cup water
½ cup vinegar
1 Tbsp. gluten-free soy sauce
⅓ cup water
¼ cup cornstarch

Mix sugar and first amount of water. Add vinegar and soy sauce. Pour over sausage. Cook in slow cooker on low for 8–10 hours or on high for 4–5 hours. Stir second amount of water and cornstarch together. Add to slow cooker. Cook on high for 15–20 minutes to thicken or pour into a large saucepan to thicken on burner.

Sunday Pork Roast

4 Tbsp. gluten-free flour mix, divided

1 tsp. salt

1 scant tsp. pepper

1 bay leaf, finely crushed

½ tsp. dried thyme

1 bone-in pork loin roast (4-5 lbs.)

2 medium onions, chopped

2 medium carrots, chopped

1 celery rib, chopped

2⅓ cups cold water, divided

⅓ cup brown sugar

Combine 2 Tbsp. flour mix, salt, pepper, bay leaf, and thyme; rub over entire roast. Place roast with fat side up in a shallow roasting pan. Arrange vegetables around roast. Pour 2 cups cold water into pan (add more water if you want a better gravy later). Bake, uncovered, at 325° for 1½ hours, basting with pan juices every 30 minutes. Sprinkle with brown sugar. Bake 30 minutes longer. Remove roast to a serving platter; keep warm. Strain pan drippings, reserving the broth. Discard vegetables. Add water to the broth to measure 1⅔ cups. Return to pan. Combine remaining flour mix and cold water until smooth; stir into pan. Bring to a boil; cook and stir for 2 minutes. Serve with the roast.

Campfire Dinner

10 large potatoes, cut up
6 large carrots, cut up
2 large onions, cut up
3 lbs. gluten-free sausage, cut in chunks
salt and pepper to taste
2 cups water

Cook over fire in cast-iron pot for about ½ hour until cooked, stirring occasionally and adding more water when needed. Serve with ketchup and sour cream. This is a delicious meal for a picnic or camping trip. We usually add a salad or raw veggies to the meal.

Baked Beans

2 cups dried navy beans
4 cups water
¼ cup ketchup
⅓ cup brown sugar
2 Tbsp. molasses
5 slices bacon, fried and torn into pieces
1 tsp. salt
½ tsp. mustard
¼ tsp. pepper

Combine beans and water in slow cooker. Cook on High for 4-5 hours, or Low for 8-10 hours. Add remaining ingredients and stir well. Cook on High for about 30 minutes to blend flavours. We usually double this recipe for our family. Very good served with rice or potatoes.

Sweet-'n-Sour Steak

steaks (as many as you need for your family)

1 cup ketchup

2 Tbsp. vinegar

1 Tbsp. honey

1 tsp. salt

1 Tbsp. mustard

2 Tbsp. lemon juice

1 onion, chopped

¼ tsp. pepper

Mix sauce together well. Pour over steaks in slow cooker and cook all day on low temperature. If steaks are frozen, cook on high for full day. This makes even the toughest cuts tender. Serve extra sauce over rice.

Lasagna

4–6 servings

Meat Sauce:

1–1½ lbs. ground beef

1 onion, chopped

1 garlic clove, crushed

8 oz. gluten-free tomato sauce

6 oz. gluten-free tomato paste

1 cup water

1 tsp. salt

1 tsp. oregano

¾ tsp. basil

½ tsp. marjoram

2 cups cottage cheese

1 egg

⅓ cup Parmesan cheese

shredded cheese

gluten-free lasagna noodles, cooked

For the meat sauce, brown ground beef, onion, and garlic. Add remaining 7 ingredients for meat sauce and simmer for 15 minutes. In a bowl, mix the cottage cheese, egg, and Parmesan cheese. In a 9x13-inch baking pan, layer in this order: 1) noodles, 2) meat sauce, 3) noodles, 4) cottage cheese mixture, 5) noodles, 6) meat sauce, 7) shredded cheese. Bake at 350° for 20–30 minutes.

Spanish Rice

4–6 servings

1 lb. ground beef

2 cups uncooked brown rice

7 cups water

1 cup gluten-free tomato paste

1 tsp. onion powder or 1 onion, chopped

2½ tsp. salt

2 tsp. chili powder

Fry ground beef until lightly browned. Add rice and fry for about 4 minutes (add oil if needed). Add remaining ingredients and simmer until thick.

Hamburger Casserole

6 servings

1 lb. hamburger

1 cup uncooked brown rice

1 cup diced carrots

1 cup finely chopped onion

2 cups gluten-free tomato paste

2¼ cups water

dash oregano, basil, garlic salt, and onion powder

1 tsp. salt

pepper to taste

2 cups boiling water

Combine the tomato paste and first measurement of water until well blended. Mix together all ingredients in casserole dish. Cover and bake at 325° for 2 hours.

Simple Shepherd's Pie

1 lb. ground beef

2 Tbsp. oil (if using extra lean beef)

½ cup onion

½ cup celery

2 Tbsp. gluten-free flour mix

1 tsp. salt

¼ tsp. pepper

1 cup boiling water

½ Tbsp. gluten-free beef bouillon powder (or 1 cube)

3 cups mashed potatoes

Fry beef, oil (if using), celery, and onion until beef is cooked through. Stir in flour, salt, and pepper. Combine boiling water and bouillon until bouillon is dissolved. Pour into meat mixture and stir until boiling and thickened. Spread in 8x8-inch glass pan. Cover with potatoes. Bake uncovered at 350° for half an hour. We triple this recipe for our family.

Shepherd's Pie

4–6 servings

8 medium potatoes, peeled and quartered

8 medium carrots

2 Tbsp. butter

¼ cup milk

¼ tsp. salt

1 lb. ground beef

1 medium onion, chopped

2 cups water

1 (6 oz.) can gluten-free tomato paste

2 tsp. basil leaves

1 tsp. salt

¼ tsp. paprika

1 bay leaf

2 cups frozen peas

grated cheese

Steam or boil the carrots and potatoes until soft. Mash together with butter, milk, and first measurement of salt. Brown the ground beef in a skillet, adding the onion when half browned. Add water, tomato paste, basil, salt, paprika, bay leaf, and peas to beef. Simmer for 20 minutes. Remove bay leaf and pour into 9x13-inch baking pan. Top with mashed vegetables. Bake uncovered at 350° for 30 minutes. Top with grated cheese and bake 10 minutes longer.

Stuffed Mexican Corn Bread

6–8 servings

1 lb. ground beef

1 medium onion, chopped

1–2 cloves garlic, minced

3 Tbsp. taco seasoning mix (see taco seasoning mix recipe on page 29)

½ cup water

3 medium tomatoes, chopped

1 cup salsa

2 cups cooked kidney beans or refried beans

1 cup corn

1 cup shredded carrots

1 cup grated cheese

1 recipe corn bread batter (see following recipe)

Brown meat, onions, and garlic. Drain. Stir together the Mexican seasoning and water and add. Simmer. Add tomatoes, salsa, beans, corn, and carrots. Stir to mix. Transfer to a 9x13-inch casserole dish. Top with grated cheese, then with corn bread batter. Bake at 425° for 20–25 minutes or until corn bread is golden brown.

Corn Bread for Stuffed Mexican Corn Bread

1 cup gluten-free flour mix

1 tsp. xanthan gum

1 cup yellow cornmeal

4 tsp. baking powder

¾ tsp. salt

3 eggs

⅛ cup honey

1 cup milk

¼ cup oil

Stir together the gluten-free flour mix, xanthan gum, cornmeal, baking powder, and salt. Add eggs, honey, milk, and oil. Stir just until smooth.

Beefy Rice Casserole

1½ lbs. ground beef

1½ cups chopped onion

1 cup uncooked brown rice

1½ tsp. salt

1 tsp. chili powder

1 cup water

1 (156 ml.) can gluten-free tomato paste mixed with enough water to
make 2 cups (or 2 cups gluten-free tomato sauce)

Brown ground beef, drain, and turn into slow cooker. Add remaining ingredients.
Stir, cover, and cook on low for 6–8 hours or on high for 3–4 hours.

Slow Cooker Hamburger Casserole

8 servings

3 lbs. ground beef

8 medium potatoes, thinly sliced

6 medium carrots, thinly sliced

1 medium onion, thinly sliced

2 celery ribs, thinly sliced

1½ cups frozen peas

2 tsp. salt

½ tsp. pepper

1 can tomato paste

4 tsp. gluten-free beef bouillon powder

1½ cups hot water

Brown meat, drain, and turn into slow cooker. Stir in next 7 ingredients. Mix bouillon powder and hot water together and stir in tomato paste. Pour over mixture in the slow cooker and cook on low for 8–10 hours or on high for 5–6 hours.

Meat Loaf Roll

2 lbs. ground beef
2 eggs
¾ cup gluten-free bread crumbs
¼ cup ketchup
¼ cup milk
½ tsp. salt
¼ tsp. pepper
¼ tsp. dried oregano
1½ cups chopped spinach
1 tsp. salt
thinly sliced ham
thinly sliced cheese

Mix ground beef, eggs, bread crumbs, ketchup, milk, first measurement of salt, pepper, and oregano. Pat hamburger mixture into a 12x10-inch rectangle on an 18x15-inch piece of tinfoil. Arrange spinach on the hamburger to within ½ inch of the edge; sprinkle with second measurement of salt. Arrange ham on spinach. Roll up rectangle carefully, beginning at the short side and using foil to lift the meat. Press ends and edges of roll to seal. Place on a cookie sheet and bake uncovered in 350° oven for 1¼ hours. Overlap cheese on top; cook just until cheese starts to melt (about 1 minute longer).

Michelle's Meat Sauce

2 stalks celery

2 cloves garlic, diced or crushed

1 large onion

3 lbs. ground beef

2 (5.5 oz.) cans gluten-free
   tomato paste

2 cups water

¼ cup milk (optional)

3 tsp. salt

2 tsp. sugar

2 tsp. oregano

2 tsp. basil

1 tsp. marjoram

½ tsp. rosemary

2 bay leaves

½ tsp. pepper

Brown beef with onion, celery, and garlic. Add the other ingredients and simmer for ½–1 hour. Serve on spaghetti, macaroni, spaghetti squash, or rice.

Hamburgers/Meatballs

4 servings

1 lb. hamburger

½ cup dry gluten-free bread crumbs

2 Tbsp. finely chopped onion

1 tsp. salt

½ tsp. gluten-free Worcestershire sauce

1 egg

Mix well. For hamburgers, make patties and fry on hot griddle. For meatballs, roll into about twenty 1½-inch balls and place in ungreased 9x13-inch pan; bake in 400° oven for 20–25 minutes or until light brown.

Sweet-and-Sour Meatballs

4 servings

1 recipe of cooked meatballs
¼ cup honey
1 Tbsp. cornstarch
1 (13–19 oz.) can pineapple chunks
⅓ cup vinegar
1 Tbsp. gluten-free soy sauce

Mix honey and cornstarch in skillet. Stir in pineapple (with syrup), vinegar, and soy sauce. Heat to boiling, stirring constantly. Pour over meatballs and serve.

Tilly's Meatballs

1 cup ketchup
2 cups water
1 cup brown sugar
½ cup vinegar
3 lbs. ground beef, made into meatballs

Mix first 4 ingredients together. Bring to boil in saucepan. Add meatballs, close pot, and boil for about 30 minutes (until meatballs are done). Remove meatballs and add 2 Tbsp. cornstarch (with a bit of water) to sauce to thicken. Serve over rice or potatoes. (If doubling recipe: 3 cups sugar; if tripling recipe: 5 cups sugar.)

Piquant Meat Loaf

⅔ cup gluten-free bread crumbs

1 cup milk

1½ lb. ground beef

2 eggs

¼ cup finely chopped onion

1 tsp. salt

⅛ tsp. pepper

Mix all ingredients very well and pat into a 9x13-inch glass pan or a loaf pan. Spread with piquant sauce (following recipe). Bake at 350° for about 60–75 minutes, or until done.

Piquant Sauce

3 Tbsp. brown sugar

4 Tbsp. ketchup

¼ tsp. nutmeg

2-3 tsp. mustard

Combine ingredients and mix well. Spread on top of meat loaf.

Stuffed Cabbage Rolls

4 or 5 servings

12 cabbage leaves (to separate leaves from cabbage head, remove core
  and cover cabbage with hot water; let stand about 10 minutes, then
  remove leaves)

1 lb. hamburger

½ cup uncooked white rice

1 medium onion, chopped

1 tsp. salt

⅛ tsp. pepper

⅛ tsp. garlic salt

½ cup gluten-free tomato sauce

Sauce:

1½ cups gluten-free tomato sauce

1 tsp. sugar

½ tsp. lemon juice

Drain cabbage leaves after removing them from water. Mix remaining ingredients. Place about ⅓ cup hamburger mixture at stem end of each leaf. Roll leaf around hamburger mixture, tucking in sides. Place cabbage rolls seam sides down in ungreased 8x8-inch baking dish. Mix together sauce and pour over cabbage rolls. Cover and cook in 350° oven until hamburger is done, about 45 minutes. If doubling or tripling this recipe, increase baking time.

Beef with Lentils

6–8 servings

1½ cups lentils, rinsed

1 quart water

2 Tbsp. butter

2 medium onions, chopped

1 garlic clove, minced

1 lb. ground beef

2 tsp. gluten-free beef bouillon powder

2 Tbsp. brown rice

1 tsp. sugar

1 tsp. salt

1 tsp. curry powder

½ tsp. pepper

corn tortillas

Bring the water to boil in a saucepan and add the lentils. Cook 20 minutes. Drain, reserving the liquid. In a deep frying pan, sauté the butter, onions, and garlic. Then stir in the ground beef. Brown well. Stir the beef broth powder into 2⅓ cups of the reserved liquid. Add the liquid to the meat mixture; cover and simmer 10 minutes. Stir in the lentils, rice, sugar, salt, curry powder, and pepper. Bring to a boil, reduce heat, cover, and simmer for 30 minutes, or until lentils and rice are tender and liquid is absorbed (add more liquid if necessary). Serve with warm corn tortillas.

Egyptian Rice and Lentils

When we made this dish, we cooked it on the stovetop in a large pot, and then simmered it until the lentils and rice were soft and the consistency was right—approx. three hours.

1 cup brown lentils, washed and picked over

¾ tsp. salt

4½ tsp. olive oil

1 large onion, chopped

½ tsp. ground cinnamon

1 Tbsp. ground cumin

½ cup rice

5 cups water

Place the olive oil into the bottom of a crock-pot. Turn the pot onto the highest setting (if variable available) and add the onions. Allow the onions 10–15 minutes to warm in the oil. Add the remaining ingredients, including the water. If cooking the dish all day (i.e. a morning start), reduce heat to low; otherwise leave on high setting. Cover. Leave to simmer. Stir the dish while in the crock-pot. If it is dry, add a little water. If it's soup-like, remove lid for a little while, or turn heat to high setting.

Rice and Honey Lentils

2 quarts water

1¼ cups lentils, rinsed

1 cup chopped onion

2 tsp. prepared mustard

¼ tsp. salt

½ tsp. pepper

¼ tsp. ground ginger

½ cup honey

2 cups brown rice

4 cups water

corn tortillas

Bring the first measurement of water to a boil and add the lentils. Cook on low until tender (30–60 minutes). Drain lentils and combine in casserole dish with remaining ingredients. Cover and bake for 1 hour at 350°. Serve in warm corn tortillas.

Chicken Apple Casserole

5 or 6 servings

2 Tbsp. butter

3 Tbsp. minced onion

½ tsp. garlic powder

2 Tbsp. honey

1¼ cups chicken broth

2 cups apple juice

2¼ cups soft gluten-free bread crumbs, divided

3 cups diced unpeeled red apples

3 cups cubed cooked chicken

Sauté onion in butter in a skillet until soft, but not brown. Stir in the garlic powder, honey, chicken broth, and apple juice. Heat until almost boiling. Add 2 cups of the bread crumbs, the apples, and the chicken. Remove from heat and scrape into a casserole dish. Sprinkle with the remaining bread crumbs. Bake at 400° for 20 minutes.

Chicken Strata

6 servings

8 slices gluten-free bread

2 cups diced cooked chicken or turkey

½ cup chopped onion

½ cup finely chopped celery

½ cup mayonnaise

¾ tsp. salt

dash pepper

2 eggs, slightly beaten

1½ cups milk

1 recipe white sauce made with a combination of milk and chicken broth (see White Sauce recipe on page 27)

Butter two slices of bread, cut in ½-inch cubes, and set aside. Cut remaining bread into 1-inch cubes and place half in the bottom of an 8x8-inch baking dish. In a bowl, combine the chicken, onion, celery, mayonnaise, salt, and pepper. Spoon over the bread cubes. Sprinkle remaining unbuttered bread cubes over chicken mixture. Combine the eggs and milk in a bowl, and pour over all. Cover and chill for one hour or overnight. Preheat oven to 325°. Spoon the white sauce on top. Sprinkle with buttered bread cubes. Bake for 1 hour.

Chicken Pot Pie

4–6 servings

1 cup chopped onion

1 cup chopped celery

1 cup chopped carrots

½ cup chopped sweet pepper

⅓ cup melted butter

½ cup rice flour

2 cups chicken broth

1 cup milk or cream

2 tsp. salt

¼ tsp. pepper

4 cups chopped chicken or turkey

pastry dough (see pastry recipe on following page)

Preheat oven to 400°. Sauté vegetables in butter for 10 minutes. Add rice flour to vegetables and cook for 1 minute, stirring constantly. Combine broth and milk. Gradually stir into vegetables, stirring constantly until thick and bubbly. Stir in salt and pepper. Add meat, stirring well. Scrape mixture into 9x13-inch baking dish. Top with a layer of dough and cut slits in top. Bake 40 minutes.

Pot Pie Pastry

Does not work well for a dessert pastry.

1¼ cups brown rice flour
1 cup tapioca starch
½ Tbsp. sugar
½ tsp. baking soda
2 tsp. xanthan gum
½ tsp. salt
¾ cup lard
¼ cup milk

Sift together dry ingredients into bowl. Add lard and mix till texture of bread crumbs. Add milk gradually, testing texture. Dough should pull together into a nice ball. Chill for one hour if it is too soft to handle. Tape a piece of plastic wrap to the countertop, place dough onto plastic wrap, and lay a second piece of wrap on top. Roll dough to desired shape and thickness. To place on top of chicken mixture, untape wrap from counter and peel top layer off. Pick up the dough by the two far corners of the bottom layer of wrap and invert on top of the pan. Peel off the wrap and push any cracks together.

Creamed Chicken

6 servings

¼ cup butter

1 onion, chopped

¼ cup rice flour

2 cups chicken broth

1 cup milk

salt and pepper to taste

2–3 cups diced cooked chicken

Heat the butter in a heavy saucepan. Add the onion and sauté just until soft. Add the rice flour, stirring and cooking until bubbly. Add the broth, milk, and salt and pepper. Cook, stirring constantly, until smooth and thickened. Add the chicken. Heat through and sprinkle with parsley. Serve over rice or mashed potatoes.

Pineapple Chicken

1 Tbsp. honey

1 Tbsp. cornstarch

1 (16 oz.) can crushed pineapple or tidbits, with juice

¼ cup gluten-free soy sauce or Braggs liquid soy seasoning

¼ tsp. garlic powder

¼ tsp. ground ginger

chicken pieces

In saucepan, combine honey and cornstarch. Stir in remaining ingredients, except for the chicken. Cook and stir over medium-low heat until thickened. Pour half of sauce over chicken, then baste occasionally with extra sauce. Bake for 1 hour at 350°.

Fried Chicken

Coating Mix:

2 cups rice flour

1 tsp. salt

¼ tsp. pepper

½ Tbsp. thyme

½ Tbsp. tarragon

½ Tbsp. ginger

½ tsp. garlic powder

½ tsp. oregano

Heat butter in glass baking pan in 425° oven until melted. Place coated chicken in pan and bake for 1 hour, turning chicken once after 30 minutes.

Fried Cod

Use same coating mix as above, adding 1 Tbsp. dried parsley. Heat butter in glass baking pan in 450° oven until melted. Place the thawed and coated cod fillet in the butter and bake for 4–6 minutes per ½ inch of fish, until it flakes easily with a fork.

Glazed Chicken Wings

The traditional main dish for our New Year's supper.

3 lbs. chicken wings (17–18)

⅓ cup gluten-free soy sauce or Bragg's liquid soy seasoning

2 Tbsp. vegetable oil

½ Tbsp. chili powder

2 Tbsp. water

¼ cup honey

1 tsp. salt

½ tsp. ginger

¼ tsp. garlic powder

¼ tsp. cayenne pepper, optional

Mix glaze ingredients and pour over chicken. Cover and refrigerate, turning chicken occasionally, at least 1 hour. Heat oven to 375°. Drain chicken, reserving marinade. Place chicken on rack in foil-lined broiler pan. Bake 30 minutes. Brush chicken with reserved marinade. Turn chicken and bake, brushing occasionally with marinade, until tender, about 30 minutes.

Texas Fried Chicken

2 Tbsp. vinegar

4 Tbsp. water

¼ tsp. red pepper

2 Tbsp. sugar

3 Tbsp. ketchup

1 tsp. chili powder

1 Tbsp. prepared mustard

1 tsp. paprika

Put sauce over chicken pieces in roaster pan, and bake for 1 hour at 350°.

Chicken and Biscuits

1 cup chopped onion

1¼ cups peas

1¼ cups diced carrots

⅓ cup melted butter

4 cups cooked and chopped chicken

½ cup gluten-free flour mix

2 cups chicken broth (or 2 cups water with 1 Tbsp. gluten-free chicken bouillon powder)

1 cup milk

2 tsp. salt

¼ tsp. pepper

Biscuits:

2 cups gluten-free flour mix

1 tsp. xanthan gum

4 tsp. baking powder

½ tsp. salt

½ tsp. cream of tartar

½ cup chilled butter

¾ cup milk

Steam peas and carrots just until tender. Sauté onion in butter for 10 minutes. Add flour, stirring constantly with whisk. Combine broth and milk. Gradually stir into butter mixture, stirring constantly until thickened. Add salt and pepper. Stir in meat and vegetables. Put into 9x13-inch glass pan and cover with biscuit batter.

Biscuits: Stir together dry ingredients. Cut in butter; mix until crumbly. Add milk. Dab batter on top of chicken mixture—the batter will be very sticky! Bake at 350° for 30 minutes or until golden brown.

Grandma's Turkey Stuffing

1½ cups butter

1 cup chopped onion

1½ cups chopped celery

2 tsp. salt (a little less if stuffing won't be cooked in turkey)

¼ tsp. pepper

2 tsp. thyme

1 tsp. turmeric

1 tsp. sage

12 generous cups gluten-free bread cubes

Simmer all ingredients except bread cubes in butter for 10 minutes. Add to bread. Stuff turkey. Bake turkey at 325°. If you make the stuffing separately from the turkey, bake it in foil or a pan with turkey neck or wings to give it flavor.

Oven-Fried Potatoes

enough medium potatoes for your family, scrubbed and sliced into
   wedges
gluten-free seasoning salt
¼–½ cup butter

In a 10x13-inch glass pan, melt the butter at 375°. In a bowl, liberally season the potatoes with the seasoning salt and/or any other spices of your choice. Mix well. Set wedges into pan, peel side down, single layer. Bake for 1 hour or until potatoes are cooked, stirring occasionally.

Stuffed Potatoes

5 or 6 servings

7-8 medium potatoes
1 medium-large squash
¼ Tbsp. melted butter
salt or cumin, optional
parsley

Bake potatoes at 425° for 1 hour. Cook squash in steamer. Cool potatoes slightly and cut in half. Gently scrape out pulp—don't tear skin. Combine pulp, squash, and butter. Add salt or cumin if desired and mix until creamy. Heap mixture into potato skins. Brush with butter. Sprinkle on parsley. Broil for 10 minutes.

Vegetable Rice Pilaf

Mom is a great cook, especially when it comes to using up bits of vegetables and making them into something delicious! This recipe is her invention.

1 large carrot, shredded

1 cup chopped broccoli

1 cup chopped cauliflower

1 stalk celery, chopped

2 small onions, chopped

2 cloves garlic, pressed

2 cups brown rice

4 cups water

4 tsp. gluten-free chicken bouillon powder or soup base

1 tsp. salt

Sauté celery, onions, and garlic in 2 tsp. olive oil. Put into large casserole dish and add the other ingredients. Mix and bake for 45 minutes to an hour, until done.

Rice, Corn, and Cheese Casserole

3 cups cooked rice

2 cups corn (10 oz. frozen or a 15 oz. can drained)

1 small onion

2 cups grated cheddar cheese

1½ cups milk

½ tsp. salt

½ tsp. chili powder

¼ tsp. pepper

paprika

Mix all ingredients well, except paprika. Pour into casserole dish and sprinkle with paprika. Bake 40–45 minutes at 350°. If you double this recipe, double the baking time.

Auntie Jo's Zucchini Quiche

Crust:

2 cups cooked brown rice

½ cup grated cheese

1 egg

½ tsp. salt (if you boiled the rice without salt)

Filling:

3 cups grated zucchini

½ cup chopped onion

2 Tbsp. butter

½ tsp. salt

¼ tsp. pepper

1 cup grated cheese

1 cup cooked ground meat (chicken, turkey, or beef)

4 eggs

1¼ cups milk

Crust: Mix rice, cheese, egg, and salt, and pat into a greased 9x13-inch pan (a double recipe fits well into a 10x15-inch pan). Bake at 350° for 10 minutes or so.

Filling: Sauté zucchini, onion, salt, and pepper in butter until soft and moisture is all gone. Spread over rice crust. Sprinkle cheese over zucchini and then add the meat. Beat eggs and milk, and pour over meat. Bake at 350° for 55–60 minutes until puffed and golden. A knife should come out clean. (This recipe doubles well. We often make this recipe with carrots as well. Simply substitute half the amount of zucchini for grated carrots, and sauté with the other vegetables. Can be made meatless or with ham or turkey.)

Cooked Brown Rice

2 servings

   1 cup brown rice
   2 cups water
   ½ tsp. salt, optional

Variations: 1) Sauté chopped celery, onions, and carrots in olive oil or butter. Stir into cooked rice.

Variations: 2) Boil rice in 2 cups chicken or beef broth for added flavour.

My Notes

Hieberts' Gluten-Free Cooking

Breakfast

My Notes

Pancakes/Waffles

3 eggs

2 cups gluten-free flour mix

2 tsp. xanthan gum

1½ cups milk

¼ cup oil

1 Tbsp. honey

2 Tbsp. baking powder

1 tsp. salt

Beat eggs with hand beater until fluffy; beat in remaining ingredients until smooth. Pour into waffle iron or onto greased griddle. Add more liquid if batter is too thick.

French Toast

¼ cup rice flour

2 tsp. sugar

⅛ tsp. salt

1 cup milk

3 eggs

9 slices gluten-free bread

Beat first five ingredients with hand beater until smooth. Soak bread in egg mixture until saturated. Cook on hot, greased griddle until golden brown on both sides.

Kaitlyn's Favorite Breakfast

1 serving

1 piece gluten-free bread

⅓ cup fresh or thawed raspberries

⅓ cup fresh or thawed blueberries

⅓ cup vanilla yogurt

Lightly butter both sides of bread, and fry in frying pan until golden brown. Gently stir the fruit into the yogurt, and spread over the toast. Top with maple syrup, and cut up to eat. Enjoy with a bowl of cold cereal!

Crepes

1 cup gluten-free flour
pinch of salt
½ tsp. xanthan gum
2 eggs
1¼ cups milk
1 Tbsp. butter, melted

Mix the dry ingredients in a large bowl and make a well. Add eggs and half the amount of milk. Whisk into a thick, smooth batter. Then whisk in the rest of the milk and melted butter. Heat a nonstick frying pan over medium heat. Grease the pan with oil. Pour in 3 Tbsp. batter and tilt the pan so that the batter covers the base. Cook for 1–1½ minutes until golden brown underneath. Flip the crepe with a spatula (or toss it if you feel adventurous!) and cook for another minute.

This recipe makes a delicious breakfast with syrup and/or white sugar and fruit. We also like using it as a wrap for chicken and other fillings.

Brown Rice Cereal

1 serving

1½ cups brown rice flakes
pinch salt
1 cup milk
1 Tbsp. butter

Rinse the rice flakes in cold water. Then put washed flakes into a bowl and cover with cold water. Leave to soak 3–4 minutes. Drain well. In a small saucepan, stir together soaked rice flakes, salt, milk, and butter. Simmer gently for 5 minutes, stirring occasionally. Serve with light cream or milk and brown sugar.

Breakfast Millet

THE daily breakfast at the Hiebert home.

Per serving:
1 cup water
¼ cup hulled millet

Soak in pot overnight. The next morning, bring to a full boil, then reduce heat and simmer *covered* for about 20 minutes, or until water is absorbed, leaving a soft texture. Serve with milk and honey. Other options include sliced bananas, raisins, or apples.

Cornmeal

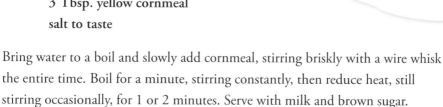

Per serving:

1 cup water

3 Tbsp. yellow cornmeal

salt to taste

Bring water to a boil and slowly add cornmeal, stirring briskly with a wire whisk the entire time. Boil for a minute, stirring constantly, then reduce heat, still stirring occasionally, for 1 or 2 minutes. Serve with milk and brown sugar.

Ultimate Oatmeal

My husband invented this breakfast—it's a winner! ~ Nicole

2 cups water

dash salt

1 cup pure, uncontaminated rolled oats (available at health-food stores)

crunchy peanut butter (avoid peanut butter sweetened with powdered sugar)

cinnamon

brown sugar

milk

Combine water, salt, and rolled oats in a saucepan and bring to a boil. Stir and reduce heat. Simmer for several minutes, then turn off heat and let sit for a minute or two before serving. To each bowlful, add a spoonful of peanut butter, a sprinkle of cinnamon, sugar, and milk.

Baked Oatmeal

6–8 servings

½ cup butter or oil

¾ cup honey

4 eggs

5 cups pure, uncontaminated rolled oats

1 cup raisins

4 tsp. baking powder

1½ tsp. salt

2 tsp. cinnamon

2 tsp. vanilla

2 cups milk

Cream butter and honey. Add eggs and beat well. Add remaining ingredients and mix. Pour into greased 9x13-inch baking pan. Bake at 350° for 30 minutes. Serve with fruit salad, yogurt, or milk. Because some of us cannot handle dairy even in baking, we simply use oil in place of butter and water in place of milk. Since we find whole rolled oats quite heavy, we often will make our own quick oats by blending the oats in a blender for a little while.

Multi-Grain Hot Cereal

A filling and delicious hot cereal!

 10 cups water
 1 cup quinoa
 ½ cup amaranth
 2 Tbsp. flaxseeds
 1 cup rice flakes
 ½ cup cornmeal
 1½ tsp. salt

Bring first 4 ingredients to a boil. Boil until soft. Add the remaining ingredients, whisking constantly until blended, thick, and cooked. Serve with milk and sugar. Makes 16 servings.

Martha's Granola

8 cups pure, uncontaminated oats
¾ cup dried, unsweetened cranberries
¾ cup chopped dates
1½ cups coconut
1½ cups slivered almonds
½ cup honey
½ cup butter

Melt butter and honey together. Stir into other ingredients and mix well in a roaster. Bake uncovered at 350° for half an hour or until evenly toasted, stirring every 8 minutes. Store in an airtight container. Serve with milk or yogurt. Very yummy and not too chewy!

Buckwheat Granola

12 cups buckwheat sprouts*

1 cup coconut

1 tsp. salt

4 tsp. cinnamon

3-4 cups chopped nuts

½ cup oil

½ cup honey

½ cup water

½ cup pitted dates

¼ cup flaxseeds

Mix buckwheat, coconut, salt, cinnamon, and nuts together in a large bowl. Put remaining ingredients in a blender and blend well. Pour into the buckwheat mixture and stir well. Either dehydrate at medium heat or bake in oven on low temperature until crispy. Store in freezer or refrigerator.

Buckwheat sprouts: Soak buckwheat for one day, then rinse and place in colander with a plate underneath, rinsing 2–3 times a day for 2 or 3 days or until sprouts are about ¼ inch long.

Sunday Morning Rice Breakfast

3 cups brown rice
6 cups water

Cook as regular brown rice. Once it is cooked, serve with raisins, coconut, sunflower seeds, sesame seeds, buckwheat granola, slivered almonds, cinnamon, honey, and milk. Makes a filling and delicious breakfast!

Breads & Muffins

My Notes

Hieberts' Gluten-Free Cooking

Bread

An old standby which has been in the family for over ten years. It's the very best bread recipe we have ever discovered.

Dry Ingredients:
6 cups gluten-free flour mix

5 tsp. xanthan gum

3 tsp. salt

3 tsp. gelatin

6 tsp. instant yeast

Wet Ingredients:
4 eggs

⅓ cup vegetable oil

⅓ cup honey

2 tsp. vinegar

½–¾ cup peeled and grated potato, raw

2½ cups warm water

Sift together dry ingredients in medium bowl. With heavy-duty mixer, blend first 4 wet ingredients. Add potato and beat. Add water, and with beaters on low, gradually add dry ingredients. Beat on highest speed for 3½ minutes. Spoon into 2 or 3 greased bread pans and let rise for 10 minutes. Bake in 350° oven for 25 minutes. Cover with tinfoil and bake for another 40 minutes. Best fresh. After two days, slice remaining bread, freeze, and use for toast. This recipe can sometimes be finicky, often depending on the weather. In some altitudes the xanthan gum may need to be increased or decreased by a teaspoon or so.

Buttery Corn Bread

⅔ cup butter, softened

½ cup honey

4 eggs

1⅔ cups milk

2⅓ cups gluten-free flour mix

2 tsp. xanthan gum

1 cup yellow cornmeal

4½ tsp. baking powder

1 tsp. salt

Cream butter and honey in large mixing bowl. Combine the eggs and milk in a separate bowl. Combine gluten-free flour mix, xanthan gum, cornmeal, baking powder, and salt in a third bowl; add to the creamed mixture alternately with the egg mixture. Pour into a greased 9x13-inch pan and bake at 400° for 22–27 minutes or until a toothpick inserted near the center comes out clean. Cut into squares and serve warm.

French Bread

3 cups gluten-free flour mix

3 tsp. xanthan gum

2 tsp. sugar

2 tsp. salt

1 Tbsp. instant yeast

3 egg whites

1 tsp. vinegar

2 Tbsp. oil

1⅓ cups warm water

Combine dry ingredients in a bowl. Mix wet ingredients in mixing bowl. Add dry ingredients and beat for 3 minutes on high. Spoon into a greased French bread pan. If you don't have a regular pan, shape tinfoil into a French bread mold and grease well. Let rise for 30 minutes. Bake at 425° for 30 minutes. Serve hot.

For an even better product, use the master mix (following recipe). Omit the xanthan gum from the original French bread recipe and decrease salt by 1 teaspoon.

Master Mix

7 cups rice flour

5 cups tapioca starch

¼ cup xanthan gum

¼ cup gelatin

½ cup sugar

Mix well and store in a cool, dry place.

Perogies

2 cups gluten-free flour mix
2 tsp. xanthan gum
1 tsp. salt
3 egg whites
¼ cup cream
¼ cup milk

Filling:
2 cups cottage cheese
3 egg yolks
salt to taste

Sift together first 3 ingredients. Make well and add other ingredients. Mix well with a spoon. Will appear sticky, but will be workable with lots of tapioca starch on rolling pin, hands, and table. Roll out on tapioca starch-covered surface. Cut into squares and fill. Cook in salted boiling water (to which a splash of vegetable oil has been added) for 5 minutes. Serve with cream sauce (thickened with cornstarch), strawberries, and a sprinkle of sugar. For a simpler option, simply leave as open,unfilled squares and serve with cottage cheese on top rather than inside.

Pizza Crust

Crust (makes 2 crusts):

3 cups master mix (recipe on page 117)

1 tsp. salt

2½ tsp. instant yeast

4 egg whites

3 Tbsp. vegetable oil

1 tsp. vinegar

1½ cups warm water (more or less)

Preheat oven to 400°. Grease 2 pizza pans. Blend the dry ingredients in a medium bowl. Set aside. Place the wet ingredients in the bowl of a heavy-duty mixer and blend. (Reserve some of the water.) Turn the mixer to low and add the dry ingredients. Add more water if necessary to get a firm dough that can still be spread. Beat on high for 3½ minutes. Spoon the dough onto the prepared pans and spread in circles about 12 inches in diameter. (Dip a spatula into oil to help with the spreading process.) Let rise about 10 minutes, then bake for 10 minutes. Add your toppings and bake again about 22–25 minutes.

Yeast-Rising Thick Pizza Crust

A very good pizza crust.

2 cups rice flour

2 cups tapioca starch

3½ tsp. xanthan gum

1 tsp. salt

2 Tbsp. dry yeast

1 cup lukewarm water, 105°–115°

1 Tbsp. sugar

3 Tbsp. shortening

½ cup hot water

4 egg whites at room temperature

Mix flours, xanthan gum, and salt in mixer bowl. Stir yeast and sugar into the warm water. Melt shortening in the hot water. Blend the dry ingredients on low. Pour in the hot water and shortening, blending to mix. Add the egg whites, blend again, then add the yeast mixture. Blend on high speed for 4 minutes. Spoon half of the dough onto a greased cookie sheet or round pizza pan. With your hand in a greased plastic bag, pat the dough out in a circle about ¼ inch thick except at the edges, which should be higher to contain the sauce and fillings. Repeat with second half of dough. Spread immediately with your sauce and favorite toppings. There is no need to let this rise, but by allowing 20 minutes of rising time you will get an even thicker crust. Bake in preheated 400° oven for 20–22 minutes. Makes two 12½-inch pizzas.

Sesame Sticks

These are very sticky to make, but they are a delicious snack!

4 eggs
1 Tbsp. sugar
½ cup oil
1¼ cups gluten-free flour mix
½ tsp. salt
½ tsp. xanthan gum
sesame seeds

Beat eggs in mixing bowl until light-colored and thick. Add sugar and oil. Beat very well. Stir flour, salt, and xanthan gum together. Add 1 tablespoon of this at a time to the egg mixture as you continue beating. Take a small ball of dough and roll into the shape of a thick pencil, 6 inches long. Roll in sesame seeds. (It works to roll out the dough through oiled plastic bags on your hands.) Arrange on ungreased pans. Bake at 350° for 25–30 minutes, until brown and crisp.

Zucchini Bread

4 eggs

4 cups shredded zucchini

3 cups gluten-free flour mix

2 tsp. xanthan gum

1 cup honey

⅔ cup oil

1 tsp. salt

1½ tsp. baking soda

1½ tsp. baking powder

2 tsp. cinnamon

2 tsp. vanilla

1 cup chopped nuts

Beat eggs well with a whisk until frothy. Add remaining ingredients and mix well with a spoon. Bake at 325° for 1 hour in 2 greased loaf pans.

Raisin-Zucchini Bread

4 eggs

2 cups white sugar

1 cup vegetable oil

3 tsp. vanilla

3 cups grated zucchini

3 cups gluten-free flour mix

3 tsp. xanthan gum

3 tsp. baking powder

¼ tsp. baking soda

1 tsp. salt

2 tsp. cinnamon

1½ cups chopped nuts

1 cup raisins

Beat together the eggs, sugar, and oil, then add remaining ingredients. Bake in 2 greased loaf pans at 375° for 1 hour.

Zucchini Coconut Loaf

2 eggs

½ cup oil

1 cup sugar

1 cup grated zucchini

½ tsp. vanilla

1½ cups gluten-free flour mix

½ tsp. baking powder

1 tsp. baking soda

½ tsp. salt

¾ tsp. cinnamon

½ tsp. nutmeg

½ cup coconut

½ cup chopped walnuts

1 tsp. xanthan gum

Beat oil, eggs, and sugar together. Stir in zucchini and vanilla. In another bowl, mix the remaining ingredients. Pour into the wet ingredients. Stir well. Pour into a greased loaf pan. Bake at 350° for 1 hour or until toothpick comes out clean. Cool in pan for 10 minutes and turn out on rack.

Cinnamon Bread

2 cups gluten-free flour mix

2 tsp. baking powder

½ tsp. baking soda

1½ tsp. cinnamon

1 tsp. salt

1½ tsp. xanthan gum

1 cup sour milk or buttermilk

¼ cup oil

3 eggs

2 tsp. vanilla

Topping:

2 Tbsp. white sugar

1 tsp. cinnamon

1 tsp. butter

Measure all ingredients in order given into large mixing bowl. Beat for 3 minutes. Pour into a greased loaf pan. Smooth top. Sprinkle with topping.

Topping: Combine all ingredients, mixing until crumbly. Sprinkle over smoothed loaf batter. Using knife, cut in a light swirling motion to give a marbled effect. Bake at 350° for about 50 minutes or until inserted toothpick comes out clean.

To make sour milk, add milk to 1 Tbsp. of vinegar to equal 1 cup. If you prefer a more cinnamony loaf, double the topping mixture.

Plain Muffins

A quick and easy complement to soup.

Dry Ingredients:
2 cups gluten-free flour mix

2 tsp. xanthan gum

½ tsp. salt

3½ tsp. baking powder

Wet Ingredients:
1 cup milk

2 Tbsp. honey

¼ cup oil

2 eggs

Preheat oven to 400°. Sift together dry ingredients in large bowl. Beat wet ingredients in smaller bowl. Pour into dry ingredients and stir well. Fill 12 greased muffin tins. Bake for 15 minutes.

Corn Muffins

Dry Ingredients:

1¼ cups gluten-free flour mix

1 tsp. xanthan gum

1 cup yellow cornmeal

¼ cup sugar or half the amount of honey

4 tsp. baking powder

½ tsp. salt

Wet Ingredients:

2 eggs

¼ cup vegetable oil

1 cup milk

Measure the dry ingredients into large bowl. Stir together and make a well in the center. Beat eggs in small bowl until frothy. Mix in oil and milk. Pour into well and stir. Fill greased muffin tins ¾ full. Bake in 400° oven for 20-25 minutes. Leave in pan for 5 minutes, then remove. Serve warm with butter. Makes 13–15 muffins.

Sunflower Seed Muffins

3 eggs

3 Tbsp. honey

1⅓ cups milk

⅓ cup oil

6 tsp. baking powder

1½ tsp. salt

1 cup pure, uncontaminated oats

2 cups gluten-free flour mix

½ cup sunflower seeds

1½ tsp. xanthan gum

Beat eggs. Add honey, milk, and oil. Combine dry ingredients. Stir into wet ingredients and mix well. Put into greased muffin tins and bake at 400° for 15 minutes. They do not brown well, so I bake them for another minute or two at 350° convection to brown them a bit. Serve hot with butter.

Banana Bread/Muffins

As soon as these muffins cool, I freeze them. I put one into my husband's lunch box the night before, and it thaws beautifully—soft and moist! ~ Nicole

¼ cup butter, softened

1 cup brown sugar

2 eggs, beaten

1½ cups gluten-free flour mix

1 tsp. xanthan gum

½ tsp. salt

1 tsp. baking powder

1 tsp. baking soda

3 bananas, mashed

½ cup walnuts, chopped

Cream the butter and sugar. Add the eggs and beat until light and fluffy. Add the flour mix, xanthan gum, salt, baking powder, and baking soda. Stir by hand. Add bananas and walnuts. Scrape into greased loaf pan and bake at 325° for 60–70 minutes, or fill greased muffin tins and bake at 400° for 20–25 minutes.

Auntie Mary Jane's Morning Glory Muffins

Very healthy and yummy!

2 cups gluten-free flour mix

1 tsp. xanthan gum

3 tsp. baking soda

2 tsp. cinnamon

½ tsp. salt

2 cups grated carrot

½ cup raisins

½ cup coconut

1 apple, peeled and grated

4 eggs

1 cup vegetable oil

2 tsp. vanilla

1 cup honey

Mix together the first 5 ingredients in a large bowl. Stir in the carrot, raisins, coconut, and apple. In a small bowl, mix the eggs, oil, vanilla, and honey. Stir wet ingredients into the dry. Fill greased muffin tins almost full. Bake at 325° for 25–30 minutes, until done.

Ginger Muffins

¼ cup butter

¼ cup white sugar or half the amount of honey

2 eggs

½ cup molasses

½ cup hot water, divided

1¾ cups gluten-free flour mix

1½ tsp. xanthan gum

1 tsp. baking soda

¼ tsp. salt

½ tsp. cinnamon

½ tsp. ginger

¼ tsp. cloves

Combine butter, sugar, eggs, molasses, and ¼ cup of the hot water in mixing bowl. Beat together well. Measure the rest of the ingredients (except for remaining hot water) into same bowl and stir together. Gradually stir hot water into batter. Fill greased muffin tins ¾ full. Bake in 400° oven for 20–25 minutes. Cool in pan 5 minutes, then remove. Makes 12 muffins.

Banana Chip Muffins

1¾ cups gluten-free flour mix

1 tsp. xanthan gum

½ cup sugar or half the amount of honey

3 tsp. baking powder

½ tsp. salt

½ cup chocolate chips

2 eggs

¼ cup vegetable oil

¼ cup milk

3 bananas, mashed

Mix first 6 ingredients in large bowl. Beat eggs till frothy. Mix in oil, milk, and bananas. Blend everything and fill greased muffin tins ¾ full. Bake in 400° oven for 20–25 minutes. Makes 12–14 muffins.

Blueberry Muffins

2 cups gluten-free flour mix

1 tsp. xanthan gum

3½ tsp. baking powder

½ tsp. salt

1 cup fresh or frozen whole blueberries

2 eggs

1 cup milk

2 Tbsp. honey

¼ cup canola oil

Preheat oven to 400°. Grease 12 medium-sized muffin cups. Stir together flour, xanthan gum, baking powder, and salt. Mix in blueberries. In separate bowl, beat eggs. Add 3 remaining ingredients and beat well. Pour wet ingredients into dry ingredients and mix together very well. Fill cups ⅔ full. Bake for 15-20 minutes or until golden brown.

Spice Muffins

2 cups gluten-free flour mix

1 tsp. xanthan gum

3½ tsp. baking powder

½ tsp. salt

1 tsp. cinnamon

½ tsp. nutmeg

½ tsp. allspice

2 eggs

1 cup milk

3 Tbsp. honey

¼ cup canola oil

Preheat oven to 400°. Grease 12 medium-sized muffin cups. Stir together flour, xanthan gum, baking powder, salt, cinnamon, nutmeg, and allspice. In separate bowl, beat eggs. Add 3 remaining ingredients and beat well. Pour wet ingredients into dry ingredients and beat together very well. Fill cups ⅔ full. Bake for 15–20 minutes or until golden brown.

Apple Streusel Muffins

1½ cups gluten-free flour mix

½ cup sugar

3 tsp. baking powder

½ tsp. salt

1 tsp. xanthan gum

2 eggs

¼ cup milk

¼ cup oil

¾ cup shredded apple

Topping:

½ cup packed brown sugar

¼ cup gluten-free flour mix

¼ cup butter

Beat eggs, milk, and oil together. Stir in apple. Mix dry ingredients together. Pour wet ingredients into dry and stir well. Fill greased muffin tins.

Mix topping together and sprinkle over muffins. Bake at 400° for 15–20 minutes.

Carrot Spice Muffins

These have become a family favorite, especially for a nutritious snack during a busy work morning!

1 ½ cups gluten-free flour mix

1 ½ cups uncontaminated quick oats

1 ½ tsp. xanthan gum

2 tsp. baking soda

½ tsp. salt

1 tsp. cinnamon

¼ tsp. nutmeg

3 eggs

¼ cup molasses

¼ cup cooking oil

¼ cup honey

1 ½ cups milk or water

2 Tbsp. vinegar

1 cup grated carrot

½ cup chopped walnuts (optional)

1 cup raisins (optional)

Combine first seven ingredients in a bowl. Beat eggs in a separate bowl. Add all remaining ingredients and stir to mix. Add to dry ingredients and mix well. Fill greased muffin cups ¾ full (batter will be quite runny). Bake at 400° for 15-20 minutes. Makes 18-20.

Cookies

My Notes

Molasses Cookies

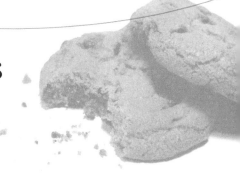

4 dozen cookies

¾ cup butter

1 cup brown sugar

2 eggs

¼ cup molasses

2¼ cups gluten-free flour mix

2 tsp. xanthan gum

½ tsp. salt

2 tsp. baking soda

1 tsp. cinnamon

1 tsp. ginger

½ tsp. ground cloves

Cream together the butter, sugar, and eggs. Add molasses. Sift together remaining ingredients and add. Mix thoroughly. Chill dough for several hours. Shape dough into balls 1 inch in diameter. (This is a sticky job…washing your hands after every 4–6 balls really helps.) Roll balls in granulated sugar and place 2 inches apart on greased baking sheet. Bake at 350° for 12–15 minutes.

Soft Molasses Cookies

6 dozen cookies

1 cup oil

1 cup white sugar

2 eggs

1 cup molasses (Tip: Measure molasses in same cup as you measured oil—it comes out easier!)

½ cup milk or water

2 tsp. baking soda

5½ cups gluten-free flour mix

5 tsp. xanthan gum

½ tsp. salt

Beat oil, sugar, and eggs together well. Add molasses. Stir milk/water and baking soda together to dissolve and add. Add flour, xanthan gum, and salt (previously mixed together). Mix well. Batter should be very sticky. Drop by teaspoonfuls onto cookie sheets lined with parchment paper. (Cookies spread, so don't place them too close together.) Bake in convection 350° oven (375° regular) for 8–10 minutes. Let cool before removing from pan. The cookies stick together, so put wax paper in between layers when putting in containers. Best if kept frozen, as they are very soft and sticky.

Dad's Cookies

1 cup butter

2 cups brown sugar

3 eggs

1 cup coconut

2 cups pure, uncontaminated rolled oats

2 cups gluten-free flour mix

2 tsp. xanthan gum

½ tsp. baking soda

1 tsp. vanilla

2 tsp. baking powder

pinch salt

Preheat oven to 350°. Cream butter and sugar together. Add eggs one at a time.
Add remaining ingredients and mix well. Roll into balls and flatten with a fork.
Bake 8–12 minutes, until nicely browned.

Double Chocolate Cookies

Soft and chewy!

1 cup + 2 Tbsp. gluten-free flour mix

1 tsp. xanthan gum

½ tsp. baking soda

½ tsp. salt

½ cup white sugar

¼ cup brown sugar

2 eggs

½ cup butter, softened

1 tsp. vanilla

½ cup chopped walnuts

1 cup semisweet chocolate chips, divided

Sift together flour mix, xanthan gum, baking soda, and salt. Add sugars, eggs, butter, and vanilla. Blend well. Melt ⅓ cup of the chocolate chips over double boiler. Cool and add to flour mixture. Stir in the nuts and remaining chocolate chips. Drop by teaspoonfuls onto ungreased baking sheet. Bake at 375° for 10–12 minutes.

Peanut Butter Chocolate Chip Cookies

I converted this recipe from one my longtime penpal in England sent me. Wow! It's our very favorite cookie! - Nicole

- ¾ cup butter, softened
- ½ cup peanut butter (avoid peanut butter sweetened with powdered sugar)
- 1 cup granulated sugar
- ½ cup brown sugar
- 1 tsp. baking powder
- ½ tsp. baking soda
- 3 eggs
- 1 tsp. vanilla
- 1¼ cups gluten-free flour mix
- 1 tsp. xanthan gum
- 2 cups pure, uncontaminated rolled oats (available at health-food stores)
- 1 cup chocolate chips

Cream together the butter and peanut butter. Add the sugars, baking powder, baking soda, eggs, and vanilla. Beat until combined, then add the remaining ingredients. Mix until combined. Drop by teaspoonfuls onto greased cookie sheets. Bake at 375° for 10–12 minutes.

Soft Raisin Cookies

About 6 dozen cookies

1 cup water

2 cups raisins

1 cup soft butter

1 cup honey or 1¾ cups brown sugar

2 eggs, lightly beaten

1 tsp. vanilla

3½ cups gluten-free flour mix

1½ tsp. xanthan gum

1 tsp. baking powder

1 tsp. baking soda

1 tsp. salt

½ tsp. cinnamon

½ tsp. nutmeg

Combine raisins and water in a small saucepan; bring to boil. Cook for 3 minutes; remove from heat and let cool (do not drain). In a mixing bowl cream butter; gradually add honey or sugar. Add eggs and vanilla. Combine dry ingredients; gradually add to creamed mixture and blend thoroughly. Stir in raisins. Drop by teaspoonfuls 2 inches apart on greased baking sheets. Bake at 350° for 12–14 minutes.

Carrot Cookies

¾ cup butter, softened

1 cup sugar

2 small eggs, beaten

1 cup cooked, mashed carrots

2 cups gluten-free flour mix

1 tsp. xanthan gum

2 tsp. baking powder

½ tsp. vanilla

Cream the first 3 ingredients together well. Stir in carrots. Stir in remaining ingredients by hand. Drop by teaspoonfuls onto greased baking sheet and bake in 350° oven for about 8–10 minutes.

Chocolate Chip Cookies

8 dozen cookies

1½ cups soft butter

1⅛ cups honey

6 eggs, beaten together very well

¾ tsp. vanilla

3 cups gluten-free flour mix

3 tsp. xanthan gum

¾ tsp. salt

¾ tsp. baking soda

6 Tbsp. cornstarch

1½ cups chocolate chips

Cream butter and honey together. Add beaten eggs. Add vanilla. Stir in remaining ingredients and mix well. Drop by teaspoonfuls onto well-greased baking sheets and bake in 350° oven for about 10 minutes.

Carob Chip Cookies

⅓ cup canola oil

½ cup honey

1 tsp. vanilla

1 egg

1¾ cups gluten-free flour mix

½ tsp. xanthan gum

1 tsp. baking soda

½ cup carob chips (unsweetened or else certified gluten-free)

dash of allspice

Oil 2 baking sheets and preheat oven to 375°. Combine oil, honey, and vanilla. Beat egg and add to oil mixture. Gradually stir in flour, xanthan gum, and baking soda to form stiff batter. Fold in carob chips and drop batter by teaspoonfuls onto cookie sheet. Bake for 10–15 minutes.

Shortbread

½ cup cornstarch

1 cup white rice flour

½ cup gluten-free powdered/icing sugar

¾ cup butter

Sift dry ingredients into bowl. Add butter with hands. Refrigerate for 1 hour. Roll into balls. Place on ungreased cookie sheet ½ inch apart. Pat down with fork. Bake at 300° for 20 minutes.

Gingerbread Cookies

Half a recipe works well and is easier on the mixer. This recipe is a favorite during the winter holidays! Spending an hour at the dining room table creating all sorts of unique people and animals is a great way of making memories!

1 cup molasses

1 cup white sugar

1 cup shortening

2 cups oriental rice flour

¼ cup cold coffee

2 eggs

3½–4 cups oriental rice flour

1 Tbsp. baking soda

2 Tbsp. cinnamon

1 Tbsp. ginger

2 tsp. xanthan gum

Mix molasses, sugar, and shortening and bring to boil over medium heat, stirring frequently. Boil for 3 minutes, stirring constantly. Pour into large bowl and allow to cool slightly. Stir in 2 cups rice flour. (The rice flour will help it cool. It should be quite warm, but not hot enough to cook the eggs when you add them.) Add coffee and eggs. Beat until smooth. Combine last 5 ingredients in a separate bowl, then gradually add to molasses mixture. Dough should be stiff, not sticky. Refrigerate dough for a short time before rolling out and cutting. Add small portion of hot water and mix again if too dry. Bake on greased cookie sheets at 350° for 4–6 minutes (small shapes 6-soft, 8-crisp; large shapes (men) 8-soft, 10-crisp). Leave cookies on pan for a few minutes until they harden. Cool and decorate with Royal Icing.

Hieberts' Gluten-Free Cooking

Royal Icing

3 egg whites
1 tsp. cream of tartar
3½ cups packed, sifted gluten-free powdered/icing sugar
few grains of salt
flavoring

Have the egg whites at room temperature. Add the cream of tartar and salt. Beat with electric mixer until mixture stands almost in peaks. Add the sugar gradually and continue beating until icing holds a stiff peak. Add flavoring. Color icing with food coloring. We like tinting it several colors in different bowls, then using chocolate chips, sparkles, raisins, and other candies to decorate our various cutouts. Icing dries out very quickly; cover unused portion with plastic wrap directly touching the icing and try to avoid bubble under the wrap.

Sugar Cookies

Another holiday favorite!

⅓ cup butter

½ cup sugar

2 tsp. baking powder

1⅛ cups gluten-free flour mix

½–1 tsp. xanthan gum

¼ tsp. salt

1 egg

½ tsp. vanilla

Cream butter; add sugar gradually until light and fluffy. Add egg and beat well.
Add vanilla. Add flour, salt, xanthan gum, and baking powder. Mix thoroughly.
Roll and cut. Bake for 10–12 minutes at 350°. Remove from pans immediately.

Brown Sugar Chews

1 egg
1 cup brown sugar
1 tsp. vanilla
¼ tsp. salt
½ cup potato starch flour
¼ tsp. baking soda
1 cup nuts, coarsely chopped or broken

Stir together egg, brown sugar, and vanilla. Add sifted flour, salt, and baking soda. Add nuts. Put in well-greased 8x8-inch pan. Bake at 350° for 18–20 minutes. (Chews should be soft inside when taken from the oven, but may be crusty on top.) Cool before cutting and removing.

Cornflake Cookies

2½–3 dozen cookies

½ cup butter, softened

½ cup white sugar

½ cup brown sugar

2 eggs

½ tsp. vanilla

2 cups gluten-free flour mix

1 tsp. baking powder

¼ tsp. salt

1 tsp. xanthan gum

½ tsp. cinnamon

¼ tsp. ginger

¼ tsp. nutmeg

⅛ tsp. cloves

1½ cups crushed gluten-free cornflakes

Cream butter and both sugars together. Beat in eggs and vanilla. Add remaining ingredients. Mix well. Drop by spoonfuls onto greased baking sheet. Bake at 350° for 10–12 minutes. You may want to try out one or two first of all to make sure the consistency is right. If it is too runny, add ½–1 cup more flour.

Hermits

4½ dozen cookies

1 cup butter, softened

1½ cups brown sugar

3 eggs

1 tsp. vanilla

3 cups gluten-free flour mix

1 tsp. baking powder

1 tsp. baking soda

½ tsp. salt

2 tsp. xanthan gum

1 tsp. cinnamon

½ tsp. nutmeg

¼ tsp. allspice

1 cup raisins

1 cup chopped dates

⅔ cup chopped nuts

Cream butter and sugar together. Beat in eggs 1 at a time. Add vanilla. Measure in remaining ingredients. Mix well. Drop onto greased baking sheets by heaping teaspoonfuls. Bake at 350° for 6–8 minutes.

These taste delicious but are very dry. If you keep them frozen they won't crumble as much. You could also try adding a banana or two.

Best Drop Cookies

5 dozen cookies

1 cup butter, softened

1½ cups packed brown sugar

3 eggs

1 tsp. vanilla

1 lb. dates, cut up

2 cups gluten-free flour mix

1 cup pure, uncontaminated oats

½ cup coconut

1 tsp. baking soda

½ cup chopped walnuts

Cream butter and sugar well. Beat in eggs and vanilla. Add remaining ingredients. Mix well. Drop by spoonfuls onto greased baking sheets. Bake at 350° for 10–12 minutes.

Oatmeal Chip Cookies

5 dozen cookies

  1 cup butter, softened
  1 cup honey
  3 eggs
  1 tsp. vanilla
  2 cups gluten-free flour mix
  1 tsp. baking powder
  ½ tsp. baking soda
  2 tsp. xanthan gum
  2 cups pure, uncontaminated oats
  2 cups semisweet chocolate chips
  ¾ cup medium coconut

Cream butter and honey together. Beat in eggs 1 at a time. Add vanilla. Add remaining ingredients. Mix well. Drop by spoonfuls onto greased baking sheets. Bake at 350° for about 8–10 minutes.

Oatmeal Raisin Cookies

3½ dozen cookies

1 cup butter, softened

1 cup brown sugar, packed

2 eggs

1 tsp. vanilla

1½ cups gluten-free flour mix

1 tsp. xanthan gum

1 tsp. baking soda

¼ tsp. salt

1¼ cups pure, uncontaminated oats

1 cup raisins

Cream butter and sugar together. Beat in eggs and vanilla. Add remaining ingredients. Mix well. Drop by spoonfuls onto greased baking sheets. Bake at 350° for 8–10 minutes.

Apple Cookies

½ cup butter, softened

¾ cup honey

2 eggs

2 cups gluten-free flour mix

1½ tsp. xanthan gum

1 tsp. baking soda

1 tsp. cinnamon

½ tsp. cloves

½ tsp. nutmeg

½ tsp. salt

1 cup peeled and grated apple

1 cup raisins

1 cup chopped walnuts, optional

Cream butter, honey, and eggs together. Mix flour, xanthan gum, baking soda, salt, and spices together and add to wet ingredients. Mix. Stir in remaining ingredients. Drop by teaspoonfuls onto greased baking sheet. Bake at 400° for 8–10 minutes.

Ranger Cookies

8 dozen cookies

1 cup butter, softened

1 cup white sugar

1 cup brown sugar

3 eggs

2 tsp. vanilla

2 cups gluten-free flour mix

1 tsp. baking soda

½ tsp. baking powder

1½ tsp. salt

2 tsp. xanthan gum

2 cups gluten-free crispy rice cereal

2 cups pure, uncontaminated rolled oats

1 cup coconut

1 cup raisins

Cream butter and both sugars together. Beat in eggs 1 at a time. Add vanilla. Stir flour, baking soda, baking powder, salt, and xanthan gum together and add to wet ingredients. Mix. Add cereal, oats, coconut, and raisins. Mix well. Dough will be thick. Roll into 1-inch balls or drop by spoonfuls onto greased baking sheets. Bake at 375° for 7 minutes. They will be very soft but will harden.

Gingersnaps

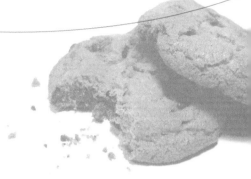

6 dozen cookies

- ¾ cup butter, softened
- 1 cup sugar
- 2 eggs
- ½ cup molasses
- 2½ cups gluten-free flour mix
- 2 tsp. baking soda
- 2 tsp. xanthan gum
- 2 tsp. ginger
- 1 tsp. cinnamon
- ½ tsp. salt

Cream butter and sugar well. Beat in eggs one at a time. Mix in molasses. Mix dry ingredients together and add. Mix well. Shape into 1-inch balls. Roll in sugar and place on greased baking sheets. Bake at 350° for 10–12 minutes.

Coconut Crisps

2½–3 dozen cookies

1 cup butter, softened
½ cup sugar
1 tsp. vanilla
2 cups gluten-free flour mix
1 cup coconut
1 tsp. xanthan gum
½ tsp. nutmeg (optional)
½ tsp. allspice (optional)
½ tsp. cinnamon (optional)
½ cup chopped walnuts (optional)

Cream butter, sugar, and vanilla together. Add dry ingredients. Mix together to form a ball. Form into small balls. Place on greased cookie sheets. Press with a fork. Bake at 350° for 15 minutes. Optional: Dip into chocolate or glaze with chocolate frosting. These are rather crumbly, but work well if kept frozen. You could try adding an egg.

Peanut Butter Cookies

4–6 dozen cookies

- 1 cup butter, softened
- 1 cup brown sugar, packed
- 1 cup white sugar
- 3 eggs
- 1 cup gluten-free peanut butter
- 3 cups gluten-free flour mix
- 2 tsp. xanthan gum
- 2 tsp. baking soda
- ¼ tsp. salt

Cream butter and sugars together. Beat in eggs 1 at a time. Mix in peanut butter. Stir in flour, baking soda, salt, and xanthan gum. Shape into small balls. Place on ungreased cookie sheets allowing room for expansion. Press with a fork dipped into white sugar. Bake at 375° for 12–15 minutes.

Raisin Cookies

1 cup butter

1½ cups sugar

1½ cups milk

2 tsp. vanilla

4 cups gluten-free flour mix

4 tsp. xanthan gum

3 Tbsp. baking powder

1 tsp. cinnamon

2 cups raisins

Cream butter and sugar. Mix in milk and vanilla. Add remaining ingredients. Bake at 375° for about 10 minutes on lightly greased pans.

Pumpkin Cookies

½ cup butter or margarine, softened

1¼ cups brown sugar

3 eggs

1 tsp. vanilla

1 cup pumpkin (cooked and mashed)

2 cups gluten-free flour mix

4 tsp. baking powder

½ tsp. salt

1½ tsp. xanthan gum

½ tsp. cinnamon

½ tsp. nutmeg

¼ tsp. cloves

¼ tsp. ginger

1 cup raisins (optional)

1 cup chopped nuts (optional)

Cream butter and sugar together well. Beat in eggs 1 at a time. Add vanilla and pumpkin. Stir remaining ingredients together and add. Mix well. Drop by tablespoonfuls onto a greased cookie sheet. Bake at 375° for about 15 minutes or until lightly browned. Makes 5½ dozen.

Marshmallow Cookies

Another favorite from Grandma!

> 4 gluten-free toffee bars or a few bags of gluten-free toffee bits
> 1 can Eagle Brand milk
> ½ cup butter
> 2–3 packages gluten-free marshmallows
> gluten-free Rice Krispies or other crispy rice cereal

Melt toffee in a double boiler. Add milk and butter; heat and stir until smooth. Dip marshmallows into toffee mixture using a fork, then coat with Rice Krispies or other crispy rice cereal. Allow to cool on cookie sheets covered with wax paper. These freeze well.

Unbaked Cookies

½ cup honey

½ cup milk

½ cup butter

¼ cup cocoa

1 cup coconut

1 tsp. vanilla

3 cups pure, uncontaminated oats

Boil first 3 ingredients for 1 minute. Remove from heat. Add remaining ingredients and stir well. Drop by spoonfuls onto wax paper-lined pans. Freeze.

For a more unhealthy cookie, omit honey and add 1 cup white sugar. The finished product just about melts in your mouth!

Honey Oatmeal Cookies

3 dozen cookies

¾ cup butter, softened

½ cup white sugar

½ cup honey

2 eggs

1 tsp. vanilla

2 cups pure, uncontaminated oats

1¼ cups gluten-free flour mix

1 tsp. baking soda

½ tsp. salt

1 tsp. xanthan gum

1 cup raisins

Cream butter, sugar, and honey together well. Beat in eggs 1 at a time; add vanilla. Stir in remaining ingredients and mix well. Roll into 1½-inch balls and set on baking sheets lined with parchment paper. Do not flatten. Bake at 350° for 12–15 minutes.

Vanilla Cookies

1 cup butter

2 cups brown sugar

4 eggs

2 tsp. vanilla

1 cup sour cream

4 cups gluten-free flour mix

3 ½ tsp. xanthan gum

1 tsp. baking soda

1 tsp. baking powder

Caramel Icing:

½ cup butter

1 cup brown sugar

½ cup milk

1¾–2 cups gluten-free powdered/icing sugar

Cream butter and sugar. Add eggs and vanilla. Add dry ingredients alternately with sour cream. Drop onto greased pan. Bake for 8 minutes at 375°.

Icing: Melt butter in saucepan over low heat. Add brown sugar and stir for 3 minutes, stirring constantly. Stir in milk and bring to a boil. Remove from heat and cool. Add powdered/icing sugar until spreading consistency.

Cakes & Desserts

My Notes

Gingerbread Cake

¼ cup butter

1½ cups gluten-free flour mix

1 tsp. xanthan gum

¼ cup granulated sugar

1 tsp. baking powder

¼ tsp. baking soda

¼ tsp. salt

¼ tsp. cloves

1–2 tsp. ginger

1 tsp. cinnamon

2 eggs, beaten

½ cup milk

½ cup molasses

Preheat oven to 350°. Put butter in a 9-inch round cake pan and place it in the oven for a few minutes until the butter melts. Combine the flour mix, xanthan gum, sugar, baking powder, baking soda, salt, and spices in a large bowl. In a separate bowl, combine the eggs, milk, molasses, and melted butter. Stir this mixture into the dry ingredients. Pour the batter into the cake pan and bake for 30–40 minutes or until a toothpick comes out clean. Serve with whipped cream.

Silver White Cake

A good basic white cake.

       2 cups gluten-free flour mix
       1½ tsp. xanthan gum
       1½ cups granulated sugar
       3½ tsp. baking powder
       1 tsp. salt
       ½ cup butter
       1 cup milk
       1 tsp. vanilla
       5 egg whites

Heat oven to 350°. Grease one 9x13-inch pan or two 9-inch round cake pans, and dust with rice flour. Beat everything except the egg whites in large mixer bowl on low speed for 30 seconds. Beat on highest speed, scraping bowl occasionally, for 2 minutes. Add egg whites and beat on high speed for 2 minutes, scraping bowl occasionally. Pour into pan(s). Bake until toothpick comes out clean (oblong pan 35–40 minutes, layers 30–35 minutes). Cool.

Rhubarb Cake

Cake:

1 ½ cups brown sugar

½ cup butter, softened

2 eggs

2 cups gluten-free flour mix

2 tsp. xanthan gum

¼ tsp. salt

1 tsp. baking soda

1 cup sour milk or buttermilk

1 tsp. vanilla

2½ cups rhubarb, diced in small pieces

Topping:

½–1 cup chopped nuts

¼ cup brown sugar

1 tsp. cinnamon

Cream together brown sugar and butter until fluffy. Beat in eggs. Mix together flour mix, xanthan gum, salt, and baking soda. Add alternately with the sour milk to creamed mixture, beginning and ending with the flour. Stir in vanilla and rhubarb. Pour into greased and floured (with rice flour!) 9x13-inch baking pan. Mix together topping ingredients. Sprinkle over batter in pan. Bake at 375° for 40–50 minutes or until cake springs back when lightly pressed with finger.

Quicker-than-Quick Chocolate Cake

1½ cups gluten-free flour mix

1 tsp. xanthan gum

¼ cup cocoa

1 tsp. baking powder

1 tsp. baking soda

¼ tsp. salt

1 cup water

⅓ cup oil or butter, melted

¼ cup vinegar

1 tsp. vanilla

½ cup honey

Sift dry ingredients in ungreased 8x8-inch cake pan. Make well in center. Add remaining ingredients and mix until blended. Bake in 350° oven. Test with toothpick for doneness. Ice with favorite gluten-free icing and serve.

Apple Coffee Cake

Dry Ingredients:
1⅓ cups gluten-free flour mix

1 tsp. xanthan gum

3 tsp. baking powder

¼ tsp. salt

¼ cup butter, softened

Wet Ingredients:
2 eggs, beaten until frothy

¾ cup milk

1 tsp. vanilla

⅓ cup soft honey

2 cooking apples, peeled and chopped

Topping:
⅓ cup packed brown sugar

½ tsp. cinnamon

Combine dry ingredients (except butter) in large bowl. Cut or rub in butter until crumbly. Make a well in the center. In another bowl, mix together 4 wet ingredients. Pour into well and add the apples. Stir well. Scrape into greased 8x8-inch pan. Mix topping together and sprinkle over top of cake. Bake in 350° oven for 50–60 minutes or until it begins to shrink from edge of pan. Doubles well, but use only 3 eggs.

Apple Dapple Cake

4 eggs

2 cups white sugar

1 cup vegetable oil

3 cups gluten-free flour mix

3 tsp. xanthan gum

¾ tsp. salt

1¼ tsp. baking soda

1 tsp. cinnamon

4 cups shredded apples

2 tsp. vanilla

½ cup raisins

1 cup coconut

Mix and beat the eggs, sugar, and oil. Sift dry ingredients and add to egg mixture. Add apples, vanilla, raisins, and coconut. Scrape into greased 9x13-inch baking pan and bake at 350° for 35–45 minutes.

Moonlight Cake

Our grandma converted this amazing recipe to gluten-free, and it's become a family favorite!

- 10 egg whites
- 7 egg yolks
- ½ tsp. salt
- 1 tsp. cream of tartar
- 1½ cups granulated sugar
- 1 cup rice flour
- ½ tsp. xanthan gum
- 1½ tsp. vanilla

Sift rice flour before measuring, then sift 5 times. Sift sugar 5 times. Place egg whites and salt in large bowl and beat at medium high speed until frothy, about 1 minute. Add cream of tartar and continue beating until egg whites are stiff, but not dry. This requires about 2 ½ minutes. Very gradually add the sugar to the egg whites. This takes about 1 minute. In a small bowl, beat egg yolks until creamy, about 1 minute. Using a metal spoon, fold yolks and vanilla into whites, then fold in the rice flour and xanthan gum, adding only a few tablespoons at a time. Rinse a 5½x10-inch tube pan with cold water before putting in the batter. Cut down through the batter with a wide spatula to remove any large air bubbles. Bake in 325° oven for 60–65 minutes. When removed from the oven, invert pan on wire cake cooler until cold. When thoroughly cooled, carefully remove from pan by loosening cake from sides of pan with a knife.

Pumpkin Cake

We used this recipe for our wedding cake! ~ Nicole

1½ cups gluten-free flour mix

1 tsp. xanthan gum

2 tsp. baking powder

1½ tsp. cinnamon

1 tsp. baking soda

½ tsp. salt

½ tsp. nutmeg

¾ cup honey

⅔ cup milk

½ cup oil

3 eggs

1 cup cooked pumpkin

Whisk together first 7 ingredients in bowl. Add remaining ingredients all at once and beat thoroughly. Pour into greased 9x13-inch pan and bake at 350° until center springs back, 20–30 minutes. If doubled, only use 5 eggs. Ice with gluten-free cream cheese icing.

Sweet Potato Cake

¼ cup butter

1¼ cups gluten-free flour mix

¾ tsp. xanthan gum

½ cup honey

2 tsp. cinnamon

1 tsp. baking soda

½ tsp. salt

2 egg whites

¾ cup cooked and mashed yam

1 (8 ¾ oz.) can undrained crushed pineapple

1 tsp. vanilla

1 cup chopped nuts

Melt butter in an 8x8-inch pan. Add remaining ingredients; mix with wooden spoon. Bake at 325° for 40–45 minutes. Doubling recipe can also make 2 small loaves of bread.

Best Chocolate Cake

A very basic chocolate cake that isn't too chocolaty.

 1 cup gluten-free flour mix

 1 cup sugar

 ½ tsp. baking soda

 ½ tsp. salt

 ¼ tsp. baking powder

 ½ tsp. xanthan gum

 ¼ cup plus 2 Tbsp. water

 ¼ cup plus 2 Tbsp. buttermilk (add 1 tsp. vinegar to regular milk to make buttermilk)

 ¼ cup shortening

 2 eggs

 ½ tsp. vanilla

 ⅓ cup semisweet chocolate chips or 2 squares baking chocolate, melted in a double boiler and cooled

Beat all ingredients together in a large mixing bowl on low speed for 30 seconds, scraping bowl constantly. Beat on high speed for 3 minutes, scraping bowl occasionally. Pour into a greased and floured 8x8-inch glass pan. Bake at 350° for 30–35 minutes, until a toothpick comes out clean.

Vanilla Butter Frosting

3 cups gluten-free powdered/icing sugar
⅓ cup butter or margarine, softened
1 ½ tsp. vanilla
2–3 Tbsp. milk

Mix powdered/icing sugar and butter. Stir in vanilla and milk; beat until frosting is smooth and of a spreading consistency, adding more milk or powdered/icing sugar as needed.

Chocolate Butter Frosting

⅓ cup butter or margarine, softened
⅓ cup semisweet chocolate chips, melted and cooled (or 2 squares baking chocolate)
2 cups gluten-free powdered/icing sugar
1½ tsp. vanilla
2–3 Tbsp. milk

Mix butter and chocolate. Stir in powdered/icing sugar. Beat in vanilla and milk until frosting is of a spreading consistency, adding more milk or powdered/icing sugar as needed.

Jelly Roll

Our grandma was famous for her gluten-free goodies…this jelly roll was almost her trademark!

¾ cup potato starch flour
1 tsp. baking powder
¼ tsp. salt
¾ cup granulated sugar
4 eggs
1 tsp. vanilla
gluten-free powdered/icing sugar
jelly, whipped with a fork

Beat eggs and sugar in top of double boiler until lukewarm. Remove from heat and beat with electric mixer until thick and creamy. Add vanilla. Gradually add potato starch with baking powder and salt. Pour into large shallow pan (11x15-inch), lined with greased wax paper. Bake at 350° for 20–25 minutes (until it looks done). Remove from pan, placing it on a cloth sprinkled with powdered/icing sugar. Take off paper and trim off edges. Spread with jelly or prepared pie filling. Roll up quickly and wrap in towel until cake cools. (You do have to work fast or cake will crack as it cools.)

Cream Puffs

I have fond memories of eating cream puffs stuffed with Cool Whip and strawberries at Grandma's dining room table in the evening! Eating gluten-free was grand! – Nicole

½ cup water
¼ cup butter
¼ tsp. vanilla
⅛ tsp. salt
7 Tbsp. rice flour
2 eggs

In a saucepan, bring water, butter, vanilla, and salt to a boil over medium-high heat. Stir in rice flour all at once and stir until mixture is smooth and forms a ball. Remove from heat. Cool 5 minutes. Add eggs, one at a time; mix batter until smooth. Drop by large spoonfuls onto baking sheet. Bake at 400° for 30–35 minutes, until golden brown and crisp. Cool on rack.

Baked Chocolate Pudding

1 cup gluten-free flour mix

1 tsp. xanthan gum

½ cup sugar

4½ tsp. cocoa

½ tsp. salt

2 tsp. baking powder

2 Tbsp. melted butter

½ cup milk

1 tsp. vanilla

½ cup sugar

½ cup brown sugar

⅓ cup cocoa

1 cup water

Stir together the flour mix, xanthan gum, first measurements of sugar and cocoa, salt, and baking powder. Add the butter, milk, and vanilla, and stir well. Spread into a greased 8x8-inch baking pan. Mix the sugars and cocoa together and sprinkle over top of cake. Pour the water over whole cake. Do not mix. Bake at 350° for 30 minutes and serve with ice cream.

Marshmallow Squares

¼ cup butter

4 cups gluten-free miniature marshmallows (or 40 regular-sized)

½ tsp. vanilla

5 cups gluten-free cornflakes or Rice Krispies

Melt butter, add marshmallows, and cook until dissolved and well blended. Remove from heat and add vanilla. Then add cornflakes/Rice Krispies. Pat into greased pan. We occasionally add peanuts, raisins, and sunflower seeds to make it more interesting. A few tablespoons of peanut butter added to the hot marshmallow mixture is another option.

Favorite Pastry

2¼ cups gluten-free flour mix

1 tsp. salt

1 Tbsp. sugar

1 tsp. xanthan gum

¾ cup shortening

1 egg, lightly beaten

2 Tbsp. apple cider vinegar

2 Tbsp. cold water

Mix dry ingredients. Cut in the shortening. Blend together the beaten egg, vinegar, and cold water. Stir them into the flour mix. Knead into a ball—the dough won't toughen. Separate into two balls and roll between two sheets of wax paper—tape bottom piece to the counter to prevent it from sliding around. Remove top sheet, invert dough on hand, and lay into pie pan. Remove bottom sheet and press dough into pan, smoothing any cracks or holes. Repeat with other crust or use as the top crust. Prebake the crust at 450° for 10–12 minutes. Fill pie crust and follow baking directions for filling recipe.

Grandma's Apple Pie Filling

10 cups peeled apples, sliced small

3½ Tbsp. minute tapioca

2 cups sugar

¾ tsp. Everfresh

½ cup water

Mix apples with 1½ cups of sugar and Everfresh and let stand till juice forms. Boil this mixture for 2 minutes. Add ½ cup water, ½ cup sugar, and tapioca. Boil 3 minutes longer. Cool. Make pies or freeze.

Banana Bombe

Another favorite from Grandma's kitchen! 8 servings. Freezing time: 4 hours or overnight.

1 square semisweet chocolate, melted

2 ripe bananas, mashed

1½ cups cold milk

1 tsp. vanilla

1 package (102 grams) gluten-free vanilla instant pudding mix

1 package (250 grams) Philadelphia cream cheese (soft—room temperature)

1 tub (500 mL) Cool Whip, thawed

Line a glass bowl with plastic wrap. Drizzle inside with melted chocolate. Chill. Mash bananas. Set aside. Put milk, vanilla, pudding powder, and softened cheese in large bowl. Beat on medium speed until smooth. Stir in bananas. Fold in Cool Whip. Spoon into chilled bowl. Freeze until firm. Remove from freezer, unmold, and remove plastic wrap. Place on serving plate. Let stand at room temperature 5 minutes or so before slicing to serve.

Strawberry Dessert

1 gluten-free white cake, prebaked
gluten-free vanilla pudding
whipped cream, sweetened
fresh strawberries, sliced

Spread the pudding over the cake, followed by the whipped cream. Top with fresh strawberries.

Ice Cream Cake

1 gallon ice cream
1 large container Cool Whip
1 package gluten-free Oreo-type cookies

Let ice cream and Cool Whip soften. Mix them together in a large bowl until well mixed. Blend the cookies in a blender—the amount will vary with how many crumbs you want. If you like chunky ice cream cake, blend them for less time. Mix into ice cream mixture. Spoon into a large flat container or glass pan. Freeze. This makes a very large amount, so we normally cut it in half for our family and get a full 9x13-inch glass pan. One very yummy variation is adding fresh strawberries, washed and blended up like the cookies. A family favorite!

Trifle

This is one of my favorite desserts. I first made it at my graduation supper and it's been a hit with our entire family ever since, even with the ones who don't really like chocolate.
~ Brianne

a 10x13-inch pan gluten-free chocolate cake (I like using Best Chocolate Cake)

1 quart gluten-free vanilla pudding

1 or 2 containers Cool Whip (depending on how much you like you can also use whipped cream, but since I'm dairy-intolerant, this is my substitute)

1 quart strawberry sauce, sweetened and thickened with cornstarch gluten-free chocolate syrup

Cut the cake into small squares. Line the bottom of a large glass bowl with half of the cake. Spoon half of the strawberry sauce over the cake and cover with half of the pudding. Spread half of the Cool Whip over the pudding. You can put some chocolate syrup on top of the Cool Whip here if you want. Layer the rest of the cake over the Cool Whip and top with more strawberries and pudding. Spread the Cool Whip over the top of the pudding, sealing off the edges of the bowl. Top with remaining strawberries. Drizzle chocolate syrup over the whole—and serve!

Banana Boats

A fun campfire treat!

ripe bananas (enough for each person to have one)
gluten-free marshmallows (mini ones work best, but large ones are fine too)
chocolate bars or chips

Make a cut in the banana from the top to the bottom *without going through the bottom skin*. Stuff the banana full of chocolate squares and marshmallows. Wrap securely in tinfoil and set in coals. Let cook until chocolate and marshmallows are just melted—not too long or else it is a sticky mess. Unwrap and eat out of the peel with a spoon.

Chocolate Zucchini Cupcakes

These turn out very nicely!

½ cup sour milk

½ cup butter, softened

½ cup oil

1¾ cups granulated sugar

3 eggs

2 cups grated zucchini (peeled if too mature)

2½ cups gluten-free flour mix

2 tsp. xanthan gum

¼ cup cocoa

½ tsp. baking powder

1 tsp. salt

1 tsp. baking soda

1 tsp. vanilla

⅔ cup chocolate chips

Put everything (except chocolate chips) into large bowl and beat on high for 4 minutes. Either stir in chocolate chips with a spoon or pour batter into cupcake papers and sprinkle chocolate chips on top. Bake at 350° until done.

Vanilla Cupcakes

½ cup butter, softened

½ cup white sugar

1 cup gluten-free flour mix

2 tsp. baking powder

½ tsp. xanthan gum

¼ tsp. salt

3 medium eggs

1 tsp. vanilla

Vanilla Butter Cream Icing:

½ cup butter

1 cup gluten-free powdered/icing sugar

½ tsp. vanilla

Cream butter and sugar together and add dry ingredients. Mix. Add eggs and vanilla and beat well. Line a muffin tin with cupcake papers. Fill and bake at 350° for 18–20 minutes until risen, golden, and firm to the touch. Frost with vanilla butter cream icing.

Icing: Beat butter until soft, then beat in powdered/icing sugar 1 tablespoon at a time. Add vanilla. (For chocolate butter cream icing, cut vanilla down to ¼ tsp. and add ⅓ cup melted semisweet chocolate chips and 2 Tbsp. cocoa powder.)

Jiffy Cinnamon Rolls

2 cups gluten-free flour mix

2 Tbsp. sugar

1 tsp. xanthan gum

4 tsp. baking powder

1 tsp. salt

¼ cup cold butter

1 cup cold milk

⅓ cup butter

1 cup packed brown sugar

3 tsp. cinnamon

⅓ cup raisins, optional

Put flour, sugar, xanthan gum, baking powder, and salt in a large bowl. Cut in butter until crumbly. Make a well in the center. Pour milk in well. Stir to form soft dough, adding a bit more milk if needed. Turn out on lightly floured surface. Knead. Roll into rectangle about ⅓ inch thick and 12 inches long. Cream butter, brown sugar, and cinnamon together well. Drop 1 measuring teaspoon of sugar cinnamon mixture into each of 12 greased muffin tins. Spread the remaining cinnamon mixture over the dough rectangle. Sprinkle raisins over top. Roll up as for jelly roll. Mark first, then cut into 12 slices. Place cut side down in muffin pan. Bake at 400° for 15–20 minutes. Turn out on tray.

Glaze: To ½ cup gluten-free powdered/icing sugar, add enough milk or water to make a thin glaze. Drizzle over cinnamon rolls.

Rhubarb Crisp

4 cups rhubarb, cut up

4 cups strawberries, fresh or frozen, cut up

1 tsp. salt

3–4 cups white sugar

1½ cups gluten-free flour mix

1½ cups pure, uncontaminated oats

2 tsp. cinnamon

1 cup butter, softened

Place rhubarb and strawberries in a large glass pan; sprinkle with salt. Mix the dry ingredients together and add the butter, mixing until mixture is crumbly. Spread over rhubarb. Bake at 350° until topping is golden brown and rhubarb mixture is bubbly, about 40–60 minutes. Serve warm with ice cream.

Zucchini Cake

4 eggs

1 cup oil

1¾ cups white sugar

1 tsp. salt

3 cups gluten-free flour mix

3 tsp. xanthan gum

1 tsp. baking powder

¾ tsp. baking soda

2 cups grated zucchini

Blend together the eggs and oil, then add remaining ingredients. Scrape batter into greased 9x13-inch baking pan and sprinkle with cinnamon. Bake at 350° for 1 hour and 10 minutes.

Frozen Strawberry Dessert

2 egg whites

1 cup sugar

2 Tbsp. vanilla

1 cup whipping cream

1¾ cups frozen strawberries

Beat egg whites until lightly stiff. Add sugar and vanilla. Beat until well mixed. Beat whipping cream until just thickened. Fold into egg white mixture. Add blended strawberries and mix well. Freeze for 2–4 hours in a flat dish or until set.

Apple Squares

6 Tbsp. butter

3 eggs

1 cup sugar

1 tsp. baking soda

1 tsp. vanilla

¼ tsp. cinnamon

1 cup gluten-free flour mix

1 tsp. xanthan gum

2 apples, peeled and chopped

½ cup chopped walnuts

Combine butter, eggs, sugar, baking soda, vanilla, cinnamon, flour, and xanthan gum in a large bowl. Beat until well mixed. Add apples and nuts. Mix well. Scrape into greased square glass pan. Bake at 350° for 40–50 minutes. Cool for 15 minutes. Sift powdered/icing sugar on top and cut into 36 squares.

Chewy Nut Bars

¼ cup butter

1 cup brown sugar, packed

½ tsp. vanilla

2 eggs

¾ cup gluten-free flour mix

1 tsp. baking powder

¼ tsp. salt

¾ tsp. xanthan gum

½ cup walnuts, finely chopped

½ cup chocolate chips

Melt butter; remove from heat. Stir in sugar and vanilla. Add eggs. Beat until well blended. Measure in flour, baking powder, salt, and xanthan gum. Stir. Scrape into greased 8x8-inch pan. Sprinkle nuts and chips over top. Press with hand to ensure sticking. Bake at 350° for 30–40 minutes, until set in center. Cool. Cut into 25 squares.

Gluten-Free Graham Crackers

3 cups gluten-free flour mix

1½ tsp. xanthan gum

1½ tsp. salt

1 rounded tsp. cinnamon

2½ tsp. baking powder

¾ cup butter

¼ cup honey

1 cup brown sugar

1 tsp. vanilla

⅛–¼ cup water

Whisk together flour mix, xanthan gum, salt, cinnamon, and baking powder. In a separate bowl, beat butter, honey, sugar, and vanilla. Add dry ingredients alternately with the water, using just enough water to make dough that handles easily. Refrigerate for at least 1 hour. Preheat oven to 325°. Grease 2 (12x15½-inch) pans. Using half of the dough (add cornstarch if necessary), work into a ball that isn't sticky. Roll out on cornstarch-dusted plastic wrap to a rectangle ⅓ inch thick. Transfer to pan. Roll out dough till it covers the sheet ⅛ inch thick. Cut into 3-inch squares. Prick each square with a fork 5 times. Bake for 30 minutes, watching carefully that it doesn't burn. You might need to remove outer crackers if too brown.

My Notes

Dairy

My Notes

Hieberts' Gluten-Free Cooking

Yogurt

1 gallon milk
2 Tbsp. gelatin
¼ cup yogurt (we usually use vanilla flavored)

Heat milk until almost boiling. Meanwhile, fill sink with cold water. When milk is hot, mix gelatin in a bowl with water until liquid, then pour into milk. Stir well with slotted metal spoon until dissolved. Set pot in cold water to cool it quickly. Cool down to 110°. Remove pot from sink; add yogurt and stir in well. Cover and set at the back of the stove for 4 hours, keeping pot fairly warm (but not hot). Pour into large container or pail and refrigerate for at least 12 hours. Remove top layer of yogurt if necessary; blend before adding 4 cups thawed or fresh fruit and honey to taste. Blend well. Lasts in fridge for a week. The hotter your milk gets in the process, the thicker your yogurt will be.

Chocolate Pudding

1¼ cups honey
1 gallon milk
1½ cups cornstarch
1 cup cocoa
¼ cup butter
1 tsp. vanilla

Pour honey into large pot. Pour in milk. Heat until boiling. While milk is heating, blend cornstarch and cocoa in blender with some cold milk to mix. Once milk is boiling, pour mixture quickly into pot and stir constantly until it boils again. Strain through a sieve into a large bowl. Add butter and vanilla. Cool with wax paper on top. Whip before serving.

Vanilla Pudding

1¼ cups honey

1 gallon milk

1½ cups cornstarch

6 eggs

¼ cup butter

2–3 tsp. vanilla

Pour honey into large pot. Pour in milk. Heat until boiling. While milk is heating, blend cornstarch and eggs in blender with some cold milk to mix. Once milk is boiling, pour mixture quickly into pot, stirring constantly until it boils again. Strain through a sieve into a large bowl. Add butter and vanilla. Cool with wax paper on top. Whip before serving.

Milk Moos

1 gallon milk
1½ cups honey
⅔ cup cornstarch
8 cups fruit (fresh or thawed, but not mashed)

Pour honey into large pot and pour milk over top. Heat over medium heat until boiling point (do not stir). Mix cornstarch in some milk on the side until dissolved, and whisk into milk. Bring back to boil, stirring constantly. Once it boils again, remove from heat. Cool until warm. We divide the moos between two ice cream pails and stick it in the freezer to cool for about an hour. Remove film on top and stir in fruit.

Canning & Preserves

My Notes

Pickled Beets

When we sold one of our houses, our realtor gave us a jar of these pickled beets. We enjoyed them so much we asked him for the recipe!

Amount: 2 pints. Multiply according to your needs.

2 lbs. beets
water to cover

Brine:
1½ cups white vinegar
½ cup water
2 cups granulated sugar
½ tsp. table salt
mixed pickling spice and 6 cloves tied up in a double layer of cheese
    cloth for a spice bag
2 cloves for each jar

Cook beets in water to cover until tender. Cool until they can be handled. Peel and cut up. Pack into hot sterilized jars to within 1 inch of the top. Put 2 cloves in each jar.

Brine: Bring vinegar, water, sugar, and salt to a boil over medium heat in saucepan. Remove from heat. Put pickling spice bag in brine and let boil another 1½ minutes. Remove bag. Pour brine over beets to fill jar to within ¼ inch of top. Seal. Serve chilled.

Grandma's Dill Pickles

Brine:

10 cups water

1 cup vinegar

1 cup sugar

½ cup pickling salt

1–2 Tbsp. pickling spice

Boil together. Fill jars with dill, cucumbers, horseradish, green pepper, 1 clove of garlic per jar, and lastly, more dill. Fill jars with hot brine. Put on seals and lids. Place in canner. Bring to a boil until bubbles come to top or pickles discolor (10 minutes or so).

Salsa

Makes 9 small jars.

- ½ lb. jalapeno peppers (leave in veins and seeds if spicier flavor is desired)
- 3 cups banana peppers or green peppers
- 2 cups onions
- 1 cup red peppers
- 1 cup yellow peppers
- 2 (5½ oz.) cans tomato paste
- 1 Tbsp. pickling salt
- 1 tsp. dried oregano
- 8 cups tomatoes (some of the juice and seeds removed—cut open and squeeze)
- 2 cups vinegar
- 4 cloves garlic
- 2 Tbsp. sugar (or 1 Tbsp. honey)
- 2 tsp. paprika
- ¼ cup parsley

Mix vinegar and tomato paste together. Blend garlic cloves and jalapeno in blender with some of the tomato paste/vinegar mixture. Cut up the rest of the vegetables to desired size. Mix together and cook for 30 minutes. Seal in hot jars.

Grandma's Zucchini Relish

11 cups zucchini, peeled and ground up

2 large onions

1 green pepper

1 red pepper

2½ cups vinegar

4 cups sugar

1 Tbsp. turmeric

2 Tbsp. celery seed

2 Tbsp. prepared mustard

½ tsp. pepper

1 tsp. nutmeg

1 Tbsp. cornstarch

Grind zucchini, onions, and red and green peppers in food processor. Add 5 Tbsp. salt. Mix and let stand overnight. Next morning drain and rinse thoroughly in cold water. Add the rest of the ingredients. Cook 30 minutes, stirring continually. Put into hot jars and seal.

Grandma's Apple Pickles

Syrup:

1 pint honey to 4 pints water

Fill jars with crab apples. Add hot brine. Boil for 10 minutes in canner until skins are cracking.

Canned Potatoes

A real time-saver for busy days and a great way to use up all the little potatoes from your garden!

washed small potatoes (or chopped larger ones)
pickling salt

Fill ½-gallon jars with potatoes and add 2 tsp. pickling salt to each jar. Boil in canner for 4 hours.

Canned Beans/Carrots

1 gallon water
3½ tsp. pickling salt
3 Tbsp. sugar or 1½ Tbsp. honey
7 tsp. lemon juice

Fill jars with beans or carrots. Pour hot brine over them. Process for 1 hour for quart jars.

For a really easy way of canning beans and carrots, fill quart jars with vegetables, sprinkle with 1 tsp. of salt, and top with hot water. Process for 1 hour.

Canned Peaches

Syrup:
3 pints water
1 pint honey

Let the peaches sit for about a minute in hot water to loosen the skin. Peel and slice the peaches into clean quart jars. Pour hot syrup into jars until peaches are covered. Process for 9 minutes.

Canned Cherries

Syrup:
3 pints water
1 pint honey

Stem cherries and pack into quart jars. Fill jars with hot syrup. Process for 9 minutes.

Miscellaneous

My Notes

Hot Apple Cider

A favorite for cold winter days.

   2 quarts apple juice
   1 stick cinnamon
   ¼ cup honey, to taste
   3 Tbsp. lemon juice
   ¼ tsp. nutmeg

Bring apple juice and cinnamon stick to boiling point; lower heat and let simmer for 10 minutes. Add remaining ingredients and allow to simmer for at least 5 minutes longer.

Egg Shake

A quick protein snack that tastes good and has endless varieties!

   ¾ cup milk
   ¼ tsp. vanilla
   ½–1 banana (preferably frozen)
   1 egg
   honey to taste

Blend all together in blender until smooth. Makes 1 serving. You can add strawberries, raspberries, blueberries, or any other combination of fruit you feel like adding to create a rainbow of options!

Nut Mixture

For a quick snack on the go…

> 2 cups assorted nuts (peanuts, pecans, whole/slivered almonds, sunflower seeds, walnuts, etc.)
> ¼–½ cup raisins
> 2 Tbsp. gluten-free soy sauce or Bragg's liquid soy seasoning

Stir and let stand for 5 minutes. Spread on cookie sheets covered with parchment paper. Bake at 300° for 10 minutes, stirring twice. Do not overbake!

Stuffed Mushrooms

A favorite addition to our traditional New Year's meal!

1 lb. medium mushrooms

1 small onion, chopped (about ¼ cup)

½ small green pepper, chopped (about ¼ cup), optional

3 Tbsp. margarine or butter

1½ cups soft gluten-free bread crumbs

½ tsp. salt

½ tsp. thyme

¼ tsp. turmeric

¼ tsp. pepper

1 Tbsp. margarine or butter

Cut stems from mushrooms; finely chop enough stems to measure ⅓ cup. Cook and stir chopped mushroom stems, onion, and green pepper in 3 Tbsp. butter until tender, about 5 minutes. Remove from heat. Stir in bread crumbs, salt, thyme, turmeric, and pepper. Heat 1 Tbsp. butter in shallow baking dish until melted. Fill mushroom caps with stuffing mixture and place filled side up in baking dish. Bake 15 minutes at 350°. Set oven control to broil. Broil 3–4 inches from heat for 2 minutes. Serve hot.

My Notes

Index

My Notes

Hieberts' Gluten-Free Cooking

Cookies

Cakes & Desserts

Dairy

Canning & Preserves

Miscellaneous